dear
creditor

Also by Frank Kisluk:

Life After Debt—
Is Personal Bankruptcy Your Best Solution?

dear
creditor

Negotiating Your Business's Survival and Navigating its Future Success

Frank S. Kisluk, BA, CA, CIP, CFE
Trustee in Bankruptcy

Doubleday Canada Limited

Canadian Cataloguing in Publication Data

Kisluk, Frank
   Dear creditor

ISBN 0-385-25810-0

1. Corporate debt. 2. Corporate turnarounds. I. Title.

HG4028.D3K57 1999   658.15'26   C98-932847-3

Cover design by Designmode Communications Inc.
Cover illustration by Mark Harris
Text design by Kim Monteforte/Heidy Lawrance Associates
Printed and bound in Canada

Published in Canada by
Doubleday Canada Limited
105 Bond Street
Toronto, Ontario
M5B 1Y3

TRANS 10 9 8 7 6 5 4 3 2 1

CAUTION TO READER

The issues considered in this book reflect both federal and provincial statutes, as well as common law.

- Although the Bankruptcy and Insolvency Act is a federal statute and overrides all provincial law in certain areas, many decisions in a business reorganization will also be tempered by the laws applicable in your province.
- The explanations and approaches described throughout this book have been presented in the context of Ontario law, Ontario being the author's domicile. As well, the comments can reflect the law only as it exists at the time of writing.
- Although provincial laws are generally similar in purpose, the specifics may vary by jurisdiction.
- Every business, whether an incorporated company or a proprietorship, has issues particular to its own circumstances that must be considered when committing to a particular path of restructuring.

For the above reasons, I urge the reader to consult with his or her accountant, lawyer or trustee in bankruptcy prior to coming to any conclusion or committing to any course of action.

February 1999

CONTENTS

Acknowledgements ix

Foreword xi

Introduction 1

1   The Diagnostic Checkup 3

2   What You Need to Know 7

3   Role of the Trustee in Bankruptcy 25

4   Cover Your Assets 29

5   Restructuring Without a Formal Proposal . . . 39

6   The Formal Proposal 43

7   The Proposal Process 51

8   Phoenix Techniques 67

9   The Self-Employed Professional 77

10   Bankruptcy 89

11   Definitions 93

Case Studies   99

    Dr. Gordon Smith (medical doctor)   101

    Robert Bond (chartered accountant)   107

    XY Computer Services Inc. (corporation) . . .   113

Appendix   119

ACKNOWLEDGEMENTS

Although writing a book is very much a private affair, there are always those friends and colleagues in the background who participate directly and indirectly in the culmination of the work. I am particularly thankful for the quiet support of my wife, Marilyn, and my daughter, Michelle, from whom I have taken many hours of "quality time" to apply toward the completion of this book.

My editor, Kathryn Exner, has again brought her patience and critical eye to my writing, and her constant support helping me present complicated legal processes as readable text. I am also grateful to my colleague, Colin Boulton, Trustee in Bankruptcy, for his careful reading of the manuscript, and to those creditors who have always constructively and openly explained their positions in countless negotiations, recognizing that all parties to a negotiation must gain something from the process.

I have always learned from the debtors for whom I have structured settlements. So many have gone on to success and I thank them for trusting me to help.

FOREWORD

The publication and sales of *Life After Debt – Is Personal Bankruptcy Your Best Solution?* confirmed my perception that until then, there had been a void in Canadian literature that dealt with personal financial problems. Although many books had been written to help people invest their money, few were directed toward helping individuals escape severe financial distress. Similarly, very little exists with respect to financial problems in business.

I had been planning to write a book that could help business people deal with their financial problems, but I needed a focus and it came to me during a radio phone-in talk show on February 27, 1997, on which I was a guest. That very day, Eaton's had filed for bankruptcy protection, and the host asked what I thought about this. I explained that the same type of protection sought by Eaton's was also available to smaller businesses and individual entrepreneurs in Canada. This assistance exists within special reorganization provisions of the Bankruptcy and Insolvency Act.

Following the program, I decided the most important help I could offer to business owners would be to explain the options available to them to gain bankruptcy protection, similar to that obtained by Eaton's and other large corporations – information that could help them reorganize their businesses for survival.

This book reflects the lessons that I have learned through working with hundreds of businesses and self-employed professionals over the past thirty years. Their mistakes and failures follow certain patterns and, too often, can be predicted to occur and recur. It is equally true that those failures can often be prevented, or at least their severity reduced, if problems are identified before they become unmanageable.

This book is directed to you, the entrepreneur, the owner/manager of your own business. Its message is simple and straightforward: under the right conditions, together with prudent planning and appropriate professional input, you can regain control of your business and finances from your creditors and you can save your business.

While I was organizing the material for this book, one principal refrain appeared – that all business decisions, particularly for the financially troubled enterprise, derive from and lead to a process of negotiation.

Daily, we negotiate with ourselves (setting the date for a new diet, stopping smoking), our families (setting a child's allowance, planning a family vacation), our suppliers (setting prices and payment terms), our customers (setting terms of delivery and payment) and our employees (negotiating wage rates and terms of work).

Negotiating with creditors on behalf of your business is, in many ways, an extension of those types of daily negotiations. The main difference is that, unlike the many small issues negotiated daily, confronting your creditors while in financial distress usually results in your business either succeeding or failing. I will show you how to negotiate with your creditors for success.

This book is not about bankruptcy (although formal bankruptcy proceedings may sometimes be employed in a business restructuring, as outlined in Chapter 8). This book is about rebirth – saving the best of your business and resolving, once and for all, the debt problems that you and your business are facing.

INTRODUCTION

In order to confront, attack and overcome your company's financial problems, you must:

1. Conduct an honest examination of the health of your business. You must first be satisfied that your business is intrinsically sound and that the relief sought from creditors will result in a viable and profitable enterprise. That will require a careful appraisal of the basic components of your business (Chapter 1).
2. Seek out the professional help required to assist you in assessing your situation and then developing and implementing your reorganization plan (Chapter 3).
3. Determine the resources available, both internal and external, with which you can attempt to satisfy your creditors (Chapters 6 and 7).
4. Sell the plan to your creditors (Chapter 7).

It is important that you understand the implications of any special rights you have granted to creditors (secured creditors) and the statutory rights that some creditors possess at law (trust claims and preferred creditors). These are reviewed in Chapter 2.

1

I have also included a discussion of certain special restructuring techniques which can be employed along with, or as an alternative to, a formal proposal to creditors.

Protecting your personal exposure to business creditors' claims is examined in Chapter 4 and since a large percentage of businesses are unincorporated, a separate chapter is devoted to their restructuring (particularly for self-employed professionals – Chapter 9).

I have also reproduced, as an appendix, the section of Part III of the Bankruptcy and Insolvency Act that deals with Division I proposals (which are defined in Chapter 6). As you are reading this book, you may wish to refer to the statute for more specific details and wording of the relevant laws and rules.

1

—

The Diagnostic Checkup

Anyone driving an old car has, at some time, probably taken that car to a mechanic for a checkup. Ostensibly, the purpose of that visit was to determine the repairs necessary to keep the car running. A critical component of that checkup, however, was really a cost-benefit analysis. The car's owner was also determining whether the cost of the necessary repairs made economic sense when compared to disposing of the old car and buying a new one.

In much the same way, your ailing business should be subjected to a cost-benefit analysis. Can you continue to drive the business to future profits and still afford to satisfactorily settle its outstanding obligations to creditors? The future financial benefits of continued business operations must be great enough to justify the cost of a settlement with your creditors. As with that old car, paying too high a price for that future may mean that future will not last very long. There is an appropriate price for every solution, and your challenge, when considering a formal settlement with creditors, is to determine whether that price can be realistically paid by you and your business and whether it's worth the price.

In order to determine if the prospects for your business are realistically good, you must first project how the business would run if it had no financial problems. With no financial problems, could you make the business grow profitably, or would you simply fall back into the same difficulties you are now facing?

When I am approached to help a business that is in financial difficulty, the first question I ask is "Does the business operate profitably?" This may sound foolish; if the business were profitable, you might assume that it wouldn't be in trouble. But there is a world of difference between operating profitably on a day-to-day basis and being able to pay all outstanding business debts on time, as required. For example, a company may have experienced financial difficulties during a startup period, then lost money for several years and is now finally operating profitably. But the debts accumulated during the startup may be overwhelming and straining the available working capital, causing ongoing cash-flow problems. Or a business may have gone through a major market adjustment and suffered the loss of a large sector of its customer base. Although the company may have downsized to

4

compensate for that loss, the operating losses from the adjustment period still exist on the books, represented by overdue accounts payable. So even if the new streamlined company appears to be operating profitably, the business may still be encountering financial pressures when dealing with its suppliers.

In these situations, it is critical to "pretend," examining the ongoing operations of the company and its ability to continue to generate profits as if there were no creditors. Would the business continue to operate viably if the debts were all resolved today? If this magical scenario could be realized, would the company be generating a surplus of cash over what it needs to operate daily? How much cash would be generated in this scenario?

Once we are satisfied that there would be positive cash flow from this "pretend" business, we can examine the amount and nature of the existing debt and consider whether we can satisfy that debt from these cash "surpluses." How can that cash be best used to address the demands of existing creditors? Is there enough cash being generated to pay creditors over a realistic period of time or must the company seek a compromise from its creditors?

This "pretend" approach is called "zero-base budgeting." Assuming a start from ground zero, can the business perform profitably, generating positive cash flow?

Assuming there is a flow of cash from this zero-base model, the next question to address is whether that cash flow, alone or in combination with other contributions, is sufficient to support a meaningful proposal to creditors that will gain their support and allow the business to carry on.

Whether you own an incorporated business or are self-employed, the above issues will be critical when contemplating a restructuring of your finances. If your business is incorporated, you will have to consider the level of salary and dividends you require in order to pay your personal living expenses. If you are self-employed, your zero-base budget will incorporate both your net earnings from your business as well as your living expenses. In either case, it may be difficult to distinguish your personal requirements from those of your business. When contemplating approaching your creditors for assistance, you must first reconcile those conflicting requirements.

2

What You Need
to Know

Although both you and your company have your own
debt structures, your creditors can be grouped into four
main categories or classes of debt: secured, Government
Trust Claims, preferred and unsecured.

Recognizing that your anticipated reorganization and
settlement of debt will be achieved through a process of
negotiation with your creditors, you must first understand
those creditors' rights and options. Each category of creditor has different rights when enforcing collection of its
debt. The options available to these categories of creditors
also differ. In order to succeed, any proposal to creditors
must be accepted by each class of creditor to whom it is
being addressed.

Let's begin our discussion by examining these classes
of creditors.

1. SECURED CREDITORS

When you or your company borrows money from any party, that lender will naturally expect to be protected if you become unable to repay the loan as agreed. If the lender is a financial institution (e.g., a chartered bank or trust company), the money being loaned is the property of its depositors and any risks associated with the loan must be offset by some form of assurance from you. Other types of lenders would be lending you their own money and would also want the same level of protection as that required by financial institutions. That protection, including the secured creditor's rights upon default by the debtor, derives from the documents supporting the security pledge. That assurance (or pledge of security) could include one or more of the following:

(a) Specific Security

Usually when the purpose of the loan is to acquire specific furniture, equipment or leasehold improvements, you will be asked, at a minimum, to pledge the assets being purchased as security for the debt, allowing the lender to seize and sell those assets if you do not pay the debt as agreed. Those assets would be specifically listed as security and the pledge incorporated into a security agreement registered with the provincial government. In Ontario, that registration is filed under the Personal Property Security Act (PPSA). All provinces in Canada have similar registries. One example of this type of security pledge will usually be seen in borrowing agreements under government-guaranteed small business loans (SBLs). In practice, this specific security is often supplemented with an additional charge over other assets (see General Security Agreement).

(b) Assignment of Book Debts

Another asset of your business often requested as security for a loan is the debts due to you by your customers – your accounts receivable. In this instance, the pledge of the accounts receivable will usually entitle your secured creditor, under agreed circumstances, to pursue collection directly from your customers. This is a direct and sometimes faster way for creditors to obtain payment than through the seizure and sale of pledged furniture and equipment.

An assignment of book debts will usually contain certain standard provisions. The examples below include modified wording selected from a typical assignment of book debts.

General Assignment of Debts
(Excerpts)

The Pledge

FOR VALUABLE CONSIDERATION, receipt whereof is hereby acknowledged,

Manufacturing Limited (hereinafter called the "undersigned") of 77 First Street, Toronto in the Province of Ontario, hereby grants, assigns, transfers and makes over unto **BEST BANK OF CANADA**, a Chartered Bank, having its Head Office in the City of Toronto in the Province of Ontario, and having a branch office at 28 First Street, Toronto, in the Province of Ontario (hereinafter called the "Bank"), all book accounts and book debts and generally all accounts, debts, dues and demands and choses in action of every nature and kind howsoever arising or secured and now due, owing or accruing or growing due, or which may hereafter become due, owing or accruing or growing due, to the undersigned, and any and all claims which the undersigned now has or may hereafter have under any policy of insurance of whatsoever nature (the whole hereinafter called the "debts"), and the undersigned further assigns and transfers to the Bank all deeds, documents, writings, papers, books of account and other books relating to or being records of the debts or by which the debts are or may hereafter be secured, evidenced, acknowledged or made payable.

Nature of the Collateral

The undersigned agrees that the debts shall be held by the Bank as general and continuing collateral security for the fulfillment of all obligations, present or future, direct or indirect, absolute or contingent, mature or not, of the undersigned to the Bank, at or through dealings with the above branch or any of its other branches, offices or agencies whatsoever whether arising from agreement or dealings between the Bank and the undersigned or from any agreement or dealings with any third person by which the Bank may be or become in any manner whatsoever a creditor of the undersigned or however otherwise arising and whether the undersigned be bound alone or with another or others and whether as principal or surety.

Remedies on Default

The undersigned expressly authorizes the Bank to collect, demand, sue for, enforce, recover and receive the debts and to give valid and binding receipts and discharges therefor and in respect thereof, the whole to the same extent and with the same effect as if the Bank were the absolute owner thereof and without regard to the state of accounts between the undersigned and the Bank and in the name of the Bank or the name of the undersigned; provided always that the Bank shall have the right at any time and from time to time to verify the existence and state of the debts in any manner the Bank may consider appropriate and the undersigned agrees to furnish all assistance and information and to perform all such acts as the Bank may reasonably request in connection therewith and for such purpose to grant the Bank or its agents access to all places where the deeds, documents, writings, papers, books of account and other books relating to or being records of the debts may be located and to all premises occupied by the undersigned.

The Bank may, without regard to the state of accounts between the undersigned and the Bank, at any time notify any or all debtors of the undersigned of this General Assignment of Debts and may also direct those debtors to make all payments on the debts to the Bank.

The undersigned undertakes and agrees to furnish and deliver to the Bank for the purposes hereof, whenever requested by any Manager or Official of the Bank, a list of all the debtors of the undersigned with the amounts owing by each and the securities therefor, and/or all the said deeds, documents, writings, papers, books of account and other books.

All moneys received by the undersigned from the collection of the debts or any of them shall be received in trust for the Bank.

The Bank may sell either by public or private sale or otherwise dispose of any or all of the debts in such manner, upon such terms and conditions, for such consideration and at such time or times as the Bank may deem expedient and without notice to the undersigned and without any liability for any loss resulting therefrom.

(c) *Section 178 Bank Act Security — Pledge of Inventory*

When a Canadian chartered bank lends money to a manufacturing or processing business, it is permitted to take a pledge of Section 178 security with respect to certain property. That property includes the raw materials used in the manufacturing or processing business, and the security interest continues to include the ensuing work in process, finished goods and even the resultant accounts receivable after the product is sold. The legal effect of this security is to give the bank full ownership of the property. With the bank's agreement, the borrower is then allowed to deal with the inventory and/or accounts receivable in the normal course of conducting business. However, if the borrower defaults under its borrowing agreement, the bank retains the right to simply seize its own property and to deal with it.

This type of security is often accompanied by a general assignment of book debts and a general security agreement.

(d) *General Security Agreement (GSA)*

It is common for a creditor lending to your business to be concerned about relying only on a pledge of specific security. After all, those pledged assets could diminish in value over time and new assets might be purchased by the business, assets that were not originally given as security because they did not exist at the time the loan was granted. Therefore, your lender will often ask for a general security agreement (GSA), which is really a floating charge over all the assets of your business (except those previously pledged to another secured creditor). This GSA will cover anything owned by the business at the time the loan was granted, as well as any assets acquired after that time. It would also cover such assets as the name of the company, prepaid expenses (such as security deposits) and even the rights of the business to sue another party. In Ontario, proper registration of this security is required under the PPSA. A GSA will usually contain certain types of provisions.

General Security Agreement
(Excerpts)

The Pledge

The Security interest is granted to the Secured Party by the Debtor as continuing security for the payment of all past, present and future indebtedness and for the payment and performance of all other present and future obligations of the Debtor to the Secured Party, whether direct or indirect, contingent or absolute; and without limiting the generality of the foregoing, specifically including the obligations of the Debtor to the Secured Party pursuant to a loan agreement and a promissory note of even date herewith and issued by the Debtor to the Secured Party.

The Assets Pledged

The Debtor grants, mortgages, charges, transfers, assigns, creates to and in favor of the Secured Party as and by way of a fixed and specific charge and as and by way of a floating charge, a security interest in the present and future undertaking, property and assets of

---

the Debtor and in all goods, chattel paper, documents of title, instruments, intangibles and securities now owned or hereafter acquired by or on behalf of the Debtor, and in all proceeds and renewals thereof, accretions thereto and substitutions therefor (hereinafter collectively called "Collateral"), including, without limitation, all of the following now owned or hereafter owned or acquired by or on behalf of the Debtor: Inventory, equipment, accounts receivable, chattel paper, documents of title, documents, securities, proceeds and intangibles.

Remedies on Default

Upon default, if the Secured Party declares that the indebtedness shall become immediately due and payable in full, the Debtor and the Secured Party shall have, in addition to any other rights and remedies provided by law, the rights and remedies of a debtor and a secured party respectively under the Personal Property Security Act and this Agreement. Secured Party may appoint any person or persons to be a receiver of Collateral. Subject to the provisions of the Instrument appointing him, any such receiver shall have power to take possession of Collateral, to preserve Collateral or its value, to carry on or concur in carrying on all or any part of the business of the Debtor and to sell, lease or otherwise dispose of Collateral. Any such receiver may, to the exclusion of all others, including the Debtor, enter upon, use and occupy all premises owned or occupied by Debtor wherein Collateral may be situate, maintain Collateral upon such premises, borrow money and use Collateral directly in carrying on Debtor's business or otherwise as such receiver shall in his discretion determine. Except as may otherwise be directed by Secured Party, all monies received from time to time by such receiver in carrying out his appointment shall be received in trust for and paid over to Secured Party.

(e) Purchase Money Security Interest (PMSI)

Sometimes a supplier may only be prepared to sell goods to you if the supplier can be given security for its debt. Even though you may already have pledged all assets to a lender for another loan, you can still protect your supplier. Your business can grant the supplier a purchase money security interest (PMSI) in the product being sold to you. This is accomplished by your supplier serving formal notice on any creditors previously secured (such as a bank that holds security over inventory), advising the secured creditors that the supplier will be selling inventory and taking back a charge against the specific product sold to you. In fact, this type of security is similar to Section 178 security (see page 12) and will continue to attach to the sold product and the resultant account receivable until it is collected by you. This security is also registered under the PPSA or similar statute in your province and gives a form of protection to a supplier whose product can be easily identified and traced to the resultant resale. An example of the required notice is shown on page 16.

If You Default

In most businesses it is not unusual to find several secured creditors registered against different assets, and sometimes against the same assets. Each of these security agreements and pledges carries with it rights to realize on certain assets in the event of financial distress.

When a business gets into financial difficulty and has trouble paying debts when due, secured creditors will be

DEAR CREDITOR

NOTIFICATION OF PURCHASE MONEY
SECURITY INTEREST
(Under the Personal Property Security Act)

TO: Those persons named in Schedule A attached

This is to notify you that Rawproducts Ltd. has or expects to acquire a purchase money security interest in the inventory of Manufacturing Ltd. and in the proceeds of such inventory. Such inventory is described by item or type as follows:

All inventory of goods, now or hereafter acquired and wherever located, including, without limitation, widgets, widget handles, widget pipes, widget hinges.

Dated this 10th day of
December, 1998.

_____

By its Solicitors

_____

per: _____

Receipt of a copy of the within notification is acknowledged this 12th day of December, 1998

Per: _____

Name:

Title:

looking to their security to protect their loans, trade accounts receivable or the balance due on equipment sold to you. They will be reviewing the realizable value of their security and comparing that value to the outstanding debt, attempting to determine the amount, if any, of their exposure should the security have to be seized and sold at distress values.

The security agreement that you signed provided for certain steps (remedies) that your creditor can take if you don't fulfill the agreed obligations. Usually the principal obligation is to make agreed debt payments in full and on time.

The rights of competing creditors to realize on assets is governed by the priority of their registrations of security rights. If two or more creditors have registered a security interest against the same asset, the right to seizure and sale would normally go first to the creditor who registered earliest.

A simple example of a process of remedies can be seen when your business misses payments on the mortgage on its owned building. Your secured creditor, the mortgagee, might pursue the following steps:

1. The mortgagee (e.g., bank or trust company) issues a letter – a written notice of default – advising that a payment has been missed and requests payment.

2. If the payment is not received within thirty days, a legal document called a Notice of Power of Sale is delivered by the mortgagee's lawyer. This document demands either full payment of all arrears and costs

related to issuance of the notice or full payment of the outstanding balance due on the mortgage, with payment to be received within a set period of time, usually about forty-five days.

3. If neither payment is received within the forty-five-day period, the mortgagee will then have the right to take possession of the property and to sell it. The proceeds of sale will be applied to pay down the balance due under the mortgage.

4. If there are surplus monies remaining after payment of the debt and related expenses, those funds will be paid to the next-ranking registered secured creditor. If no other creditors are secured on the property, the surplus will be returned to the company. If there is a shortfall and a balance still remains unpaid, which is often the case in these situations, the shortfall will remain as an unsecured debt of the company.

In this example, the creditor technically removed the secured asset, sold it and applied the proceeds of sale toward payment of its debt. This is a basic principle of realization on secured assets.

Sometimes your secured creditor may interrupt your receipt of assets. For example, a pledge of accounts receivable, either specifically or under a general security agreement, allows the creditor, upon certain defined defaults, to seize your accounts receivable and to contact your customers directly, demanding that they redirect payments to the creditor. This is called signifying accounts receivable.

Seizing Assets

If you pledged specific assets, upon default your secured creditor can seize those assets, sell them and apply the proceeds toward the debt outstanding. A single asset might be seized by a bailiff or liquidator appointed as agent for the creditor.

The Bankruptcy and Insolvency Act (BIA) provides you some limited protection against your creditor's right to appear and seize assets. If the seizure involves all or substantially all of the operating assets of the business, the creditor must give you formal notice of its intentions. This document, called a notice of intent to enforce security, must be delivered to your business before any seizure takes place. It allows you ten days to pay the debt and thereby retain the secured assets; if you don't pay the debt in that period, the secured creditor can then enforce its rights to seize and sell the assets.

In addition, case law has developed to protect you from reckless seizure. A creditor must not only give the minimum ten days' notice but also must allow reasonable time, determined by the particular circumstances, to allow you an opportunity to redeem the security by paying the debt in full. This reasonable time could vary from one day (where the security is in jeopardy and there is clearly no hope that you will raise the necessary funds) to thirty days or more (where the process of raising the funds may be well advanced or reasonably expected). In practice, ten to twenty-one days' notice appears to have become the usual period given for smaller companies. This period for repayment is presented to the company by the secured creditor issuing a letter of demand. The loan agreement will provide for issuance of this demand if a default in payment occurs. The letter of demand is issued under the loan agreement and is in addition to the notice of intent to enforce security, which is the statutory notice required by the BIA.

Appointment of a Receiver
The actual seizure of all or substantially all assets of a business is done by a receiver. A receiver is any appointed party, usually a trustee in bankruptcy, who seizes or "receives" those secured assets in accordance with the rights given the creditor in the security agreement with the company. The receiver acts for the creditor, seizing, controlling and realizing on the security. Sometimes the security consists only of equipment, furniture or accounts receivable – all assets that can be seized and liquidated. Sometimes the security includes the goodwill of the ongoing business, in which case the receiver might continue operating the business and try to sell it as a going concern, thereby maximizing the realization.

2. GOVERNMENT TRUST CLAIMS
The income taxes, Canada Pension Plan (CPP) payments and Employment Insurance (EI) payments that you withhold from your employees' wages are considered a trust that is payable to the government on a regular basis.

Your liability for these withholdings is a priority claim in a receivership, proposal or bankruptcy proceeding and this trust must be paid in full before any payments are made to other creditors.

3. PREFERRED CREDITORS

In addition to provisions dealing with the rights of secured creditors and government trust claims for amounts withheld from wages, the Bankruptcy and Insolvency Act distinguishes certain creditors (preferred creditors) whose debts must be paid before those of unsecured creditors. The main categories of preferred creditors are listed below. Accompanying each is the relevant definition from the B.I.A.

(a) Wages and Expense Reimbursement Due Employees

Wages, salaries, commissions or compensation of any clerk, servant, travelling salesman, labourer or workman for services rendered during the six months immediately preceding the bankruptcy to the extent of two thousand dollars in each case, together with, in the case of a travelling salesman, disbursements properly incurred by that salesman in and about the bankrupt's business, to the extent of an additional one thousand dollars in each case, during the same period, and for the purposes of this paragraph commissions payable when goods are shipped, delivered or paid for, if shipped, delivered or paid for within the six month period, shall be deemed to have been earned therein.

21

(b) Rent Due to Landlord

The landlord for arrears of rent for a period of three months immediately preceding the bankruptcy and accelerated rent for a period not exceeding three months following the bankruptcy if entitled thereto under the lease, but the total amount so payable shall not exceed the realization from the property on the premises under lease, and any payment made on account of accelerated rent shall be credited against the amount payable by the trustee for occupation rent.

(c) Business and Property Taxes

Municipal taxes assessed or levied against the bankrupt, within the two years immediately preceding the bankruptcy, that do not constitute a preferential lien or charge against the real property of the bankrupt, but not exceeding the value of the interest of the bankrupt in the property in respect of which the taxes were imposed as declared by the trustee.

Preferred debts receive special treatment in reorganizations and must be paid ahead of unsecured creditors.

4. UNSECURED CREDITORS

Unsecured creditors are all creditors who do not hold security and do not have any special status such as that of a preferred creditor. For a business, this category will include debts owed to trade suppliers (for inventory, services, asset purchases) who do not hold a registered security interest in the assets. In addition, personal loans from friends and family, yourself and perhaps other partners or shareholders are all unsecured debts – unless security was obtained from the company at a time when it could be legally granted (see Chapter 4). In a proposal, even Revenue Canada is an unsecured creditor with respect to GST and income taxes.

Although unsecured creditors do not have statutory priorities, remember that, in the absence of any formal stay of proceedings under the Bankruptcy and Insolvency Act, these creditors still have the right to sue for collection and then have a sheriff seize and sell your unsecured assets on their behalf. As well, they can issue a petition to bankrupt you or your company.

A LEGAL ENTITY

When we are discussing financial liabilities, it is very important to identify exactly who is really responsible for those obligations. For example, when you personally borrow money or incur debt on your personal credit card, it is usually clear that you are the party who is obligated to repay those debts, since they are personal debts. For the individual, such as a self-employed professional, carrying on business in his or her personal name or through a registered business name, the obligation is still straightforward – the debts of the unincorporated business and your personal loans and credit cards are all personal obligations.

An entrepreneur, however, can incorporate a company (e.g., Venture Limited, Venture Inc., Good Times Ltd.) to carry on his or her business. Once incorporated, the company exists as a separate legal entity, in the same way that you exist as a separate legal person. The company conducts business, buys and sells products or services and contracts debt in its own name. A creditor who lends or sells to you personally can expect repayment from you, but if the sale is made to your corporation, that corporation, and not you personally, is liable for payment. Notwithstanding that you might be the sole shareholder, sole director and manager of the company, the fact that the sale and payment obligation were made in the corporation's name determines that the liability is that of the corporation. The concept of a legal entity is extremely critical to your ability to control your business operations and to separately control and protect your personal assets.

The discussions in this book are generally directed to the incorporated company. However, most issues and the debt settlement approaches considered are equally applicable to unincorporated businesses, including professionals, and they are more fully discussed in that context in Chapter 9. See also *Life After Debt – Is Personal Bankruptcy Your Best Solution?* for information concerning personal proposals.

3

Role of the Trustee in Bankruptcy

One often hears the expression "An expert is someone from out of town." There is some truth to that statement. The people within a business deal with many daily issues and problems on an immediate basis, making decisions in a relatively closed environment. Too often, when faced with growing financial difficulties, they "don't see the forest for the trees." The "expert" has the unique advantage of coming into that closed business environment from outside and being able to look at the forest anew.

If your business is experiencing financial difficulty, I strongly urge you to consult initially with a trustee in bankruptcy. A trustee can offer wide experience as an adviser and consultant to businesses, large and small, helping them solve their financial problems. The actual service provided by most trustees focuses on the following three areas:

1. Helping the company's principals come to an honest and sound understanding of the true nature of their business and its current difficulties.
2. Helping the company's principals develop approaches to resolving the identified problems and revitalizing the integral business of the company.
3. Helping implement the agreed solution.

When you approach an experienced trustee for advice and assistance, you will be meeting with someone who has learned many lessons through working with hundreds of financially troubled businesses. In many respects, the mistakes and failures of businesses follow certain patterns and often can be predicted. However, business failure, or at least its severity, can sometimes be prevented or reduced if the problems are identified before they become unmanageable. The special role of a trustee in bankruptcy allows him or her to participate in all aspects of corporate restructuring. When you or your business first confronts financial difficulties, it is that insight, experience and understanding that you should seek out by consulting with a trustee as early as possible.

The role of a trustee in the proposal process must be clearly understood. Under the Bankruptcy and Insolvency Act, the trustee's role is to represent the interests of the creditors to whom the proposal is being addressed. This does not mean that you should withhold information when sharing details of your situation with your trustee. If you disclose all information regarding your financial problems and history, your trustee will understand the implications of those events. This will enable him or her to alert you to anticipated concerns of all creditors and possible problems well before you begin any formal proceedings.

The trustee's responsibility to creditors includes the responsibility to ensure that the provisions of the BIA are respected in the proposal process. These provisions relate to

- providing creditors with full disclosure of your current and historical financial and business circumstances,
- ensuring that all creditors are treated fairly and equitably,
- ensuring that your rights and those of your creditors are protected,
- confirming that the offer included in the proposal is meaningful, achievable, practical and will yield a better return to creditors than the alternative of bankruptcy.

When you meet with your trustee, you can expect to be advised of your rights in dealing with creditors and your creditors' rights in questioning your financial affairs. In the context of the above obligations, you should expect to receive your trustee's best efforts to help you develop and negotiate a satisfactory settlement with your creditors.

4
—

Cover Your
Assets

There is nothing improper, immoral or illegal about protecting your business and personal assets. All business
activities contain an element of risk, and it is usually your
risk capital that is at stake when you venture forth on any
commercial journey. So, to whatever extent possible, you
should plan and seek out methods that can help protect
your assets and your personal security.

The seven areas discussed below are some of the most
frequently encountered – the general principles, however,
can be applied to all business situations.

1. INCORPORATION
Any time anyone offers you a chance to limit your personal liability, consider it very seriously. By incorporating
your business, you erect a legal wall that separates your

business and its financial exposures from your personal affairs (see the discussion about legal entities in Chapter 2). Creditors sell to your corporation and expect payment from it, not from you personally. With the exception of certain personal liabilities as a director (e.g., certain government remittances and payroll liabilities), you become personally liable for the corporation's debts only when you choose to guarantee them. Protection through incorporating a limited company is relatively inexpensive to put into place and, if available, should be employed by anyone conducting business. (Provincial laws vary with respect to the availability of limited liability incorporation for professionals.)

2. HER MAJESTY – THE LINE STARTS HERE

As a director of your company, you may become personally liable for a myriad of corporate obligations. These range from liability to remit withholding taxes on payroll, including CPP and EI, to the actual payroll due employees. Many other contingent exposures such as environmental liability exist, but the majority of small owner-managed businesses usually deal with only government remittances, GST, PST and payroll liabilities. Since you are aware of this exposure, why not make sure that you will never personally have to respond to that liability by paying these government remittances and payrolls on time? In fact, you should always pay these obligations ahead of all others. That way you will not find yourself suddenly exposed to those obligations if the corporation fails and leaves these liabilities unpaid.

It is important to understand the priority position of governments in the context of making a formal proposal to creditors.

Employee Withholding Taxes

Employee withholding taxes are the monies you are required to deduct from your employees' payroll and remit to the government. They include deductions for income tax, CPP and EI. Technically, you are holding these funds in trust for the government and must pay them, usually monthly, along with your required contribution of CPP and EI.

If you are behind in remitting these deductions, the government's right to those funds stands ahead of almost every other creditor – the government comes first. Whether your reorganization involves a proposal, bankruptcy or receivership, the government's priority even comes ahead of all secured creditors.

In a proposal, one of the mandatory terms of the arrangement must be a provision to pay this trust within six months of the plan coming into effect. When the amount of unremitted withholding taxes is very large, unless an accommodation is made by Revenue Canada, funding this payment can be a major hurdle to presenting a workable offer to creditors.

Aside from protecting your personal director's liability

when the company cannot pay the amounts due, it is just as important for the company not to accumulate a large trust debt to the government that could materially reduce funds available to your unsecured creditors in a proposal.

3. LENDING MONEY TO YOUR COMPANY

"Good news, Harry! We've reviewed your company's application to the bank for the $100,000 operating loan and we've agreed to advance the funds today. The terms of the loan are as follows: there will be no security, no interest charges and the loan will be repayable when you have the extra cash to pay us. We hope you will agree to accept the loan under these terms."

Stop laughing! Did you just say that no bank would be crazy enough to make a loan under these terms?

Seriously, a banker who made that loan would be guilty of the most extreme career-limiting move possible. A bank that intended to stay in business would almost never make that loan without security over the business's assets – accounts receivable, inventory, equipment, furniture and anything else of value.

If you lend money to your company, a separate legal entity, why are you not entitled to the same protection that your banker would require from the company before lending it even one dollar? In fact, not only are you entitled to the same protection, you should demand it!

There are a number of ways to secure your shareholder's

loan. The most common is to obtain a general security agreement from your company. This GSA would be provided to support a documented loan agreement that would reflect the conditions under which the loan was being advanced – the rate of interest being charged, terms of repayment and remedies available to you upon default in payment by the company.

If your company has already borrowed from a bank and pledged all its assets as security for that loan, you should still take back a pledge of security from the company when you advance additional funds. Remember that, in case your company must be liquidated to pay the bank's debt, any surplus available after the bank is paid will be directed to the next-in-line secured creditor. Why shouldn't that person be you? As well, there may be no bank debt outstanding at a time when the company faces a financial crisis and must cease operating. Were the company forced into bankruptcy, the security that you took when advancing money to the company could put you in first position to receive the proceeds of sale of the assets, ahead of all the company's preferred and unsecured creditors.

4. PERSONAL GUARANTEES FOR YOUR COMPANY'S LIABILITIES

A characteristic of the successful entrepreneur is his or her ability to maintain a steadfast course in the face of adversity and truly believe that the obstacles being faced by the business will be overcome. That said, this steadfastness can also act as blinders, shielding the entrepreneur from the hard reality of the situation.

When it comes to personally guaranteeing a debt, whether to a secured lender or a trade supplier, it is always a good policy to treat the guarantee in exactly the same manner as if, instead of a signature on a guarantee, a cash investment were being made. If you had the cash equivalent of the guarantee, and the same security to protect you as your business is offering the creditor, would you write the cheque?

This is a very difficult decision to make, particularly for the success-driven entrepreneur, because it forces you to step back from your emotion-laden enthusiasm and independently analyze your business, even contemplating its potential for failure. Although it is a difficult analysis, it is also the most critical and positive contribution you can make to your business.

If you are truly satisfied that the business is worthy of your investment and that the level of risk associated with your personal exposure on the guarantee is acceptable to you, go ahead, sign and push forward with confidence. But if you are having doubts about the safety of your "investment," if you see the real possibility of being called on to pay that guarantee, stop, step back from the situation and carefully analyze the conditions in the business that are causing you concern.

You must be brutally honest with yourself whenever you are considering investing your personal assets in your corporation. This applies equally to investing personal cash, furniture and equipment and a personal guarantee. In each instance, you are reducing your personal financial security, and you must be satisfied that your critical analysis of the investment reflects an acceptable level of risk for you. If that risk level appears too great, you should be looking at alternative approaches to resolving the business problem.

Occasionally, it may be necessary for you to personally guarantee a corporate debt (for example, a bank loan, a major credit card held jointly in the names of the company and you personally, or a trade debt from a key supplier). Again, as with government obligations, pay these debts on time and remove the possibility that you will ever become personally liable to pay them.

The issue of personally guaranteeing a corporate debt often cannot be avoided. In a small business it is sometimes necessary to personally guarantee payment to a new supplier, even though this appears to defeat the original purpose of incorporating for limited liability. That said, be aware of the additional exposure that you are assuming and, as soon as possible, change your terms to remove this exposure. Also, as long as your guarantee is there, ensure that those accounts are fully paid when due. In fact, by treating payments of guaranteed accounts with this priority, you will find that you can remove your personal guarantee more quickly.

It is also very important to understand that, since

providing a guarantee for the company's borrowing is equivalent to advancing cash to the company, you have the legal right to take security from your company in return for the exposure assumed. In the event that you had to personally honor the guarantee, you would have rights as a secured creditor against the company's assets for the value of the amount honored personally.

5. BUSINESS LEASES

You or your company will most likely be leasing premises and equipment. When you sign any lease, do not sign in your personal capacity – always as an officer of your corporation. Whenever possible, ensure that the responsibility for the lease is with the company only. When leasing premises, always use a separate corporation (perhaps a numbered company) as the tenant and then sublease the space from that company. In today's commercial market, this business practice is not at all unusual.

6. DO YOU KNOW WHERE YOUR ASSETS ARE?

When entering into a new business as a shareholder or director, ensure that, to the extent possible, your personal assets are owned by someone other than yourself, someone who has no possible liabilities related to that business venture. This ownership could be in the name of your spouse, your partner, your children (possibly through a trust), a parent or a friend. The issue of trust is paramount here and must be resolved comfortably. Without that trust, you might as well keep your assets and the liability exposure and be in control.

It is critical that, as part of your business planning, any transfer of assets be done before investing in and operating the new venture. Asset transfers can certainly be made at any time, but in order to be effective in protecting them from challenges by creditors, ensure that you safeguard your assets at the earliest possible opportunity. You should always obtain legal advice at the time not only to ensure that the transfers can withstand attack at a later date but also to properly document the transaction.

7. PERSONAL CREDIT RATINGS

Never forget that a personal credit rating is nothing more than a collection of information in a computer. There is no magic associated with the credit-rating process. The credit card grantors maintain a central registry through a credit bureau (the largest in Canada being Equifax), and all members report information monthly about your paying habits. This information is gathered on computer and kept separately for every individual whose name appears in those credit card monthly reports.

If your business runs into serious financial problems and you become personally liable for payment of business debts (as a director or guarantor), those problems should appear only in your personal credit record. Make sure that your spouse's credit record is not associated with yours.

Have your spouse obtain separate credit cards in his or her name. Ensure that they are carefully maintained and paid promptly, resulting in an excellent (R1) rating. Your spouse should check the credit bureau to make sure that its record is correct.

In addition, your spouse should obtain supplementary cards for you. Do not use those cards – they are insurance only. If you are forced to file a personal bankruptcy (and lose your credit cards automatically), or if your business debts overwhelm you and you can no longer maintain your own cards, you will be able to continue to use your spouse's supplementary cards in an emergency. It is his or her separate credit record that stands behind those cards, and, as long as they were previously maintained properly, you will have the ability to continue to use them.

5
___

Restructuring Without a Formal Proposal

You should always attempt to restructure your finances directly with your creditors before arriving at the point when filing a formal proposal is required. Following are examples of the kinds of restructuring that may be possible in some circumstances.

1. SECURE YOUR UNSECURED CREDITORS

If your company is dependent on two or three principal creditors whose combined debt represents the bulk of your problem trade payables, consider a business plan that converts their outstanding unsecured debt into a secured loan. In return for favorable terms of repayment and continuing supply of product, your company could provide those creditors with a secured charge over assets such as equipment or accounts receivable. That secured loan could carry a series of fixed monthly payments that would allow the company to escape the pressure of paying those debts under the existing trade terms.

Naturally, this approach depends on your creditors' confidence in your company, the availability of assets to be pledged as security and, most of all, on your viable and achievable business plan that incorporates this refinancing by your creditors.

2. A GOVERNMENT-GUARANTEED SMALL BUSINESS LOAN (SBL) OR A BUSINESS DEVELOPMENT BANK LOAN (BDB)

Both these programs – government-guaranteed small business loan (SBL) and the Business Development Bank loan (BDB) – are driven by the government to assist companies in obtaining financing. Although these loans are not usually promoted as salvation for a financially troubled company, they can sometimes be fitted into your business plan. The SBL program, for example, can support a secured loan up to $250,000 on equipment and leasehold improvements, and the BDB can finance working capital. Whether your business can qualify will depend on the severity of your financial problems. Your chartered accountant is usually the most appropriate person to investigate this option for you.

3. TALKING WITH YOUR CREDITORS

Assuming that you have developed a meaningful and viable business plan, one of the most effective tools available to you in renegotiating terms with creditors is your personal involvement in and commitment to resolving your problems. Don't hesitate to meet with your major creditors and ask for accommodation. These requests could be for delays in payments, extensions of terms, abatement of interest, an absolute reduction in the amount of debt, etc. The most critical ingredient in negotiating with creditors is communication. Hiding from creditors guarantees resentment and suspicion. By talking with them, you may help them come to understand your situation so they can try to accommodate your needs.

If none of these informal approaches can be implemented, the Bankruptcy and Insolvency Act provides another potential method of survival for your business. For example, your approach to creditors may be only partially successful, and your major creditors may agree to your proposed compromise only if all other creditors accept the same compromise. In these circumstances, the only way to enforce the will of the majority on all other creditors may be through the legal process of filing a Division I Proposal, the subject of the next chapter.

6

The Formal
Proposal

THE BANKRUPTCY AND INSOLVENCY ACT:
DIVISION I PROPOSAL

In the previous chapter, we reviewed a number of informal approaches that you should first consider when approaching your creditors for financial assistance. If that kind of relief cannot be obtained, or, even if obtained, would not be sufficient to solve your problem, consideration should be directed to the Bankruptcy and Insolvency Act and its formal processes.

The BIA provides two avenues for the financially troubled enterprise – bankruptcy and the process of filing a proposal to creditors. To be eligible to file either, a debtor must be insolvent.

The Bankruptcy and Insolvency Act defines an insolvent person as a [legal] person who lives in Canada or carries on business in Canada, whose debts exceed $1,000 and

- who cannot pay his debts when due
- who has stopped paying his bills, or
- whose assets, if sold, would not generate sufficient money to pay his debts.

The term *legal person* includes incorporated businesses.

Although both the bankruptcy and proposal processes are directed toward a resolution of financial stress, there are fundamental differences between them, as illustrated in Figure 1.

Figure 1		
	BANKRUPTCY PROCESS	**PROPOSAL PROCESS**
Person with day-to-day control of assets and/or ongoing business	Trustee	Debtor
Purpose of the filing	Liquidation	Survival of the ongoing business
Payments to creditors	Net proceeds from the sale of assets	Payments as agreed to in the proposal
Result if the creditors refuse proposal	N/A	Automatic bankruptcy

In addition to the obvious benefit of avoiding bankruptcy, the most important advantage of the proposal is the opportunity it allows to retain control of your ongoing business and its assets while developing, presenting and fulfilling your proposal to your creditors. (Your trustee has a responsibility to the creditors during this period to over-see your operations and to ensure that only proper business-related expenditures are made during the period from filing until the meeting of creditors to vote on your proposal, but this function should not interrupt your ability to conduct normal ongoing business activities.)

Before preparing your proposal, one critical issue must be confronted. *If a Division I proposal is presented to creditors and they do not support and pass the proposal, the debtor will be automatically deemed to have filed an assignment in bankruptcy.* In other words, if, at the meeting of creditors to vote on the proposal, the creditors refuse your offer, you will be bankrupt at that moment and your trustee in the proposal will then continue as trustee of your (or your company's) bankruptcy.

Because of the severity of this potential failure, filing a Division I proposal is much like a two-edged sword. It requires the debtor to put forward the best plan possible and also requires the creditors to give their most serious consideration to the offer, both parties keeping in mind the poorer outcome if the proposal were refused.

Since your direction is not toward bankruptcy, but rather toward survival, our attention will be directed to settling your debts through filing a proposal under the Bankruptcy and Insolvency Act.

The BIA allows for two types of proposals to be filed. A Consumer Proposal (filed under Division II of the BIA) is a streamlined procedure available only to an individual person whose total debt (excluding the mortgage on a personal residence) is less than $75,000. (For a complete discussion of consumer proposals, see *Life After Debt, Is Personal Bankruptcy Your Best Solution?*). All other debtors, whether individuals, unincorporated or incorporated businesses, must file a proposal under Division I of the BIA.

Therefore the types of insolvent persons who could file an ordinary, or Division I, proposal would include:

- any incorporated business or
- a self-employed individual carrying on business under a registered business name or in his or her personal name. Some examples are a doctor, dentist, accountant or lawyer (see Figure 3 on page 85).

1. WHAT IS A PROPOSAL?

A proposal is any plan of compromise offered by a debtor to its creditors. The offer can range from a few cents on the dollar of debt up to full payment of that debt. Your proposal might include any of the following ingredients:

- Payment of a lump sum of cash
- Periodic fixed payments over a specified time
- Periodic payments calculated by a formula that is based on your business's performance
- An exchange of debt for equity shares in your company, perhaps offering regular dividend or interest payments and possibly redeemable at a future date for a premium

- Delivery of a defined service up to a certain value in return for a defined forgiveness of debt
- Proceeds from the sale of specified business assets

Any arrangement that makes business sense to both you and your creditors can form the basis of an agreement.

When this proposal is filed under the BIA, certain rules must be respected and followed. Some of the most important ones are listed below:

(a) The plan must be commercially viable. There is no point in offering payments that you cannot reasonably expect to make. In fact, even if creditors support an unlikely plan, the proposal will always be reviewed by the court from the point of view of public policy to ensure that it is commercially viable.

(b) The proposal must provide for certain payments to be made in accordance with priorities set out by law. These priorities can be found in the proposal documents included in the case studies that appear later in this book. The principal priorities, listed in order of payment, are

  - Secured creditors. These creditors must be paid under the terms addressed to them in the proposal or as previously arranged with them outside the proposal.
  - Outstanding obligations to Revenue Canada for amounts withheld from employee wages, where the debtor is an employer (these obligations

include income taxes and contributions to Canada Pension Plan and Employment Insurance).

- Preferred creditors such as landlord's rent arrears and outstanding obligations to employees for wages and expense reimbusement (subject to certain prescribed limits).
- The costs of administration of the proposal, including the fees and disbursements of the trustee and its solicitor.
- The remainder of the money available for distribution to unsecured creditors is usually provided to be paid pro-rata to all unsecured creditors who have filed claims with the trustee.

2. FINANCING THE BUSINESS WHILE PRESENTING THE PROPOSAL

Although not a prescribed requirement of a proposal, one other issue must be addressed when structuring your offer to creditors. Once you have advised them of your insolvency and begun the process of presenting a proposal to them, your suppliers/creditors will generally be reluctant to continue to sell to you on credit. They will, however, usually be content to support you by selling on a cash-on-delivery basis. You should expect this to be the norm until your proposal is voted on and, you hope, supported and approved. In fact, expect their reluctance to extend credit terms to continue until you have demonstrated your ongoing creditworthiness.

This contraction or loss of credit facilities from your suppliers is a very important issue that must be addressed when developing your business plan and calculating your related cash requirements for the restructured business; this plan must be presented and sold to your creditors. You must anticipate operating on a COD basis for a period of time, and this factor must be reflected in your financial projections.

As we will discuss more fully in Chapter 7, funds sufficient to continue your business must be generated from a limited number of sources, and those funds must also support the anticipated change in creditors' terms of payment from the time when you approach your creditors and thereafter.

A proposal that will win the support of your creditors requires a combination of the following:

- Understanding what your creditors think of you and your company (based on your history of dealings, both in business and personally)
- Honestly confronting the problems of your business and developing a viable recovery program
- Developing an offer that will respond to the needs of each class or type of creditor
- Presenting an offer that is credible, that can be supported by the company and that will be perceived by your creditors as more advantageous to them than your bankruptcy

You can see from the above discussion that developing a successful proposal is as much an art as it is a legal and financial process. It requires a sensitivity to the "soft issues" as well as complete honesty in the related financial assessments. There is no point offering something that is wishful thinking or that you cannot reasonably expect your creditors to accept.

7
———

The Proposal
Process

DEVELOPING A BUSINESS PROPOSAL

1. To Whom Is the Proposal Being Presented?

A proposal under the BIA is offered to those classes of
creditors to whom you choose to present an offer of
compromise. The proposal that you offer to your creditors will reflect the debt compromise required to support your projected business plan. That business plan
will direct the structure of your proposal and determine
which creditors should be included.

For example, if you have a secured creditor such as
a bank that holds security over certain key business
assets, your business plan may include continuing the
relationship with the bank and the business's obligations to it. Assuming your secured creditor is satisfied
with the proposal and the projected operations of your

business as contemplated under the proposal, it would likely be satisfied to continue with its existing rights as a secured creditor and to not be a party to your proposal. In that circumstance, your proposal might be addressed only to preferred and unsecured creditors, with a provision that you have worked out your ongoing relationship with your secured creditor outside the proposal. On the other hand, if you have several secured creditors, your proposal might include separate provisions for settling that group of debts.

A well-prepared proposal will ensure that the interests of each class or type of creditor are addressed, either by directly negotiating with the secured creditor outside the proposal or within the formal proposal document. Your trustee in bankruptcy will be a critical party to these negotiations.

2. What Can You Offer Your Creditors?

There are three sources of payments that can be offered to creditors:

(a) Internally generated cash flow,
(b) Proceeds from the sale of surplus assets,
(c) Cash received from an external source.

(a) Internally Generated Cash Flow

Assuming your zero-base budget confirms that your business is operating profitably, the positive cash flow being generated is an asset that can be used in developing an offer of settlement with your creditors.

A proposal to creditors could include a commitment to pay them a certain amount of money on a regular basis for a specified time (e.g., $2,000 per month for 48 months). The payment would be made to the trustee in bankruptcy acting in the proposal, who would then distribute those funds to your creditors. The distributions are made in accordance with the prescribed priority rankings as set out in the BIA (see examples in the case studies.)

(b) Proceeds from the Sale of Surplus Assets

Your business might own assets that are not currently being used in your operations. They could include surplus equipment, property or even an operating division that could be sold in order to generate proceeds for repayment of debt. The proceeds from the sale of those assets could be included in the offer to creditors. This type of contribution could also help persuade creditors that your company is serious about paring costs, rebuilding and strengthening its operations, and continuing in the future as their customer.

(c) Cash Received from an External Source

There is nothing more attractive to your creditors than an immediate cash payment. Often an offer of immediate cash will help you to negotiate a smaller settlement than would a promise of future payments. Therefore, you should make every effort to include an immediate infusion of cash in the offer. The source could be your personal resources, family, friends, an outside lender or an investor. Often, introducing a new investor or partner will result in creditors looking on your proposal more favorably. After all, you ran the business while it developed its financial problems – a new partner or owner will be perceived as bringing a fresh approach and renewed confidence to business operations and should add credibility to your company's plans to continue operations.

3. Selling the Proposal

Like it or not, the principal obstacles to successfully selling your proposal to creditors are your and your company's credibility. Your creditors have watched the business's problems develop while you were in charge. You have become linked to those problems.

Selling the proposal requires the highest possible level of honesty in your disclosure of the current situation, including careful analysis of the causes of the problems, the reasons your attempts to correct them failed, and a convincing argument that the steps contemplated in the proposal will correct the past and preclude repetition of those problems. Your creditors must be satisfied that the accommodation sought from them in the proposal will result in a healthy ongoing business.

And finally, they must accept that your disclosure is complete and presents the best possible result for them in the circumstances. The settlement must be more favorable to them than the bankruptcy and winding up of the company (which would be the result if the offer were refused by your creditors).

When you present your offer, you are effectively placing the final decision on the future viability of the company in your creditors' hands. They will judge its merits by asking themselves several questions:

- Does the offer yield a better payment to them than bankruptcy?
- Does the offer provide for a balanced use of working capital that will still allow the company to access the cash it needs to continue to operate profitably?
- Are the assumptions used in projecting future operations and profitability reasonable and plausible?

The most important ingredient of your proposal is credibility – not only your credibility but that of your trustee. Choose a trustee who has the experience and reputation with creditors as someone who can bring forward and negotiate a settlement that is the best deal for both the creditors and the debtor. After all, if the creditors accept a proposal from your company and allow the business to continue and prosper, they will usually want to continue to sell to it in the future. Your trustee's ability to convey a complete understanding of your present and future position is therefore critical to bringing all parties to a meeting of minds. No proposal to reduce a debtor's obligations can be wholly palatable to creditors. It is only in the context of a choice between bankruptcy and a future good customer that your arguments can be advanced, and then only in a careful and sensitive manner.

4. Presenting the Proposal to Creditors

As stated earlier, the development of your proposal entails as much art as it does legal processes. The offer which you bring to your creditors must be structured in a manner that addresses both their needs and their perceptions of your business. For example, if your creditors are mostly small suppliers with their own cash constraints, an initial cash payment will be more attractive to them than a greater payment over a longer period of time. If they are large corporations whose interests lie in future sales to your reorganized company, your offer might include retention of cash by your business at present to allow for more growth down the road and larger future debt payments to, and orders from, those suppliers.

Or, in exchange for the support of your creditors, you could offer to subrogate or postpone your priority position over the assets of your company until a certain percentage of the debt was repaid to your creditors.

In this way, you would be demonstrating your conviction that the projected business plan and the formal proposal were achievable and were therefore worthy of support by your creditors.

Presenting the proposal and negotiating its acceptance are also very much an art. Once the projected business plan and draft proposal have been prepared, you and your trustee will want to meet privately, or in groups with your largest creditors, in an attempt to gain their support for the proposal. (Remember: three weeks after you have formally filed your proposal, your creditors will be voting on whether or not to support your offer.)

Ideally, objections from your major creditors should be discussed and accommodated in a revised draft proposal that they will commit to support. In this way, the settlement will be achieved before the final papers are filed. For example, to gain their support your major creditors may require you to agree to not receive a distribution from the proposal on account of your outstanding personal loan to the company, resulting in a greater distribution to them. Another example might be a compromise that requires you to reduce your management salary and instead draw a bonus from the business based upon its financial performance.

These examples reflect honest attempts by you and your creditors to develop alternate ways to satisfy their concerns and gain their support and, at the same time, to satisfy your needs.

As discussed more fully under the Formal Procedures (page 59), the filing of either a notice of intention to make a proposal or the proposal itself will start the countdown to the creditors' meeting and the vote on the proposal. In order to pass, the proposal must be supported by a majority of the creditors voting (50% plus 1), and those supporting must also represent at least two-thirds of the dollars owed to the voting creditors. Therefore, gaining the required support should never be casually left until the vote at the meeting of creditors. Every effort must be made to gain commitments of support from the necessary numbers and dollars of creditors at the earliest time possible.

If you must commence the process by filing a notice of intention to make a proposal (page 60), you will still have some time to negotiate before filing the actual proposal documents, but you will be legally committed to a process leading to a vote in seven weeks' time. In some circumstances, an extension of the time to file a proposal can be obtained from the court, but it would not be prudent to assume that the extension will be granted.

If, on the other hand, you commence with filing the proposal directly, without having gained prior creditor support, you will have only three weeks from the filing date to win support in time for the meeting of creditors and the vote on the proposal.

Timing issues are critical to your success and they must be carefully coordinated with your trustee. The earlier that you involve a trustee in the process, the more control you will be able to exercise. And your control of the environment is a critical component in the process of reorganization and renegotiation of debt.

THE FORMAL PROCEDURES

1. Filing the Proposal

The formal process begins with the preparation (with your trustee's assistance) of the following documents:

- A statement of affairs (balance sheet)
- A list of all your creditors
- A statement of projected cash flow (based on your business plan and which will illustrate your expected ability to meet your payment commitments to the creditors under the proposal)
- Your proposal to creditors

Your trustee will deliver these documents to the Superintendent of Bankruptcy (a department of Industry Canada), and at that time your proposal will be considered to be filed. This filing will automatically create a "stay" or freeze on all creditors' rights to pursue collection from you, including any contemplated or commenced legal actions. This freeze continues until the meeting of creditors, which must be held within twenty-one days of the filing, at which time the creditors will vote on the proposal.

After filing these documents, your trustee will send

the proposal and supporting materials to all creditors listed in the proposal, along with the trustee's report on your financial situation, explaining to them why accepting the proposal is to their advantage. At that time, creditors will also be given notice of a meeting to be held within three weeks, to consider and vote on the proposal.

In presenting the proposal to your creditors, the trustee must be able to demonstrate that

(a) if the proposal is rejected and your company is thereby placed into bankruptcy, the creditors will recover less than the amount offered in your proposal, and

(b) it is reasonable for the creditors to expect your company (or you) to be able to perform as promised in the proposal.

2. Filing a Notice of Intent to Make a Proposal

Sometimes the business crisis you are facing is so immediate there is just not enough time to review and develop the detailed business plan and proposal before filing for protection from creditors. In those circumstances, there is a very effective method of claiming instant protection from creditors – the filing of a notice of intent to make a proposal. This is a one-page document that is filed through a trustee and that immediately imposes a stay of proceedings against all creditors' actions for a period of thirty days. Your trustee will immediately mail this notice to your creditors. In some circumstances, the "stay" period can be extended for one or more additional six-week periods. (When an application to the court is made to extend the thirty-day period for filing the proposal, you must be able to demonstrate that the extended stay will not cause serious harm to the position of creditors.)

The thirty-day stay also creates a buffer period during which your trustee can talk with creditors and attempt to negotiate the settlement prior to the final formulation and presentation of your proposal to those creditors.

Within ten days of filing the notice of intent to make a proposal, you must file with your trustee a statement of projected cash flow, showing your expected cash income and expenditures for the next several months. Failure to file this document within the ten-day period will automatically result in bankruptcy. Your trustee will file it with the Superintendent of Bankruptcy and provide a copy to any creditor who requests one. When filed in conjunction with a stay of proceedings, this cash-flow statement must demonstrate that, although creditors cannot pursue collection during the thirty-day stay, your business is reasonably expected to continue to operate in a manner that ensures existing creditors' financial exposure will not increase.

As a result of filing this notice, you will have a

thirty-day period to prepare your proposal and the related documents for filing. If a proposal is not filed within that thirty-day stay period or a court-approved extended period, your company will automatically become bankrupt.

3. The Meeting of Creditors to Consider Your Proposal

At the creditors' meeting, your creditors will have an opportunity to ask you questions regarding your situation and your offer. If necessary and practical, you can change and improve the proposal even at the time of the meeting. In fact, with your creditors' consent the meeting can be adjourned to a later date to allow you to continue negotiating with creditors. At the initial or reconvened meeting, a vote on the proposal will be taken. To have the proposal approved and thus make it binding on all of your creditors, you must obtain support from more than half of the number of creditors who vote. As well, those creditors supporting the proposal must represent at least two-thirds of the total dollars owed to all creditors voting. Voting can be by mail or in person at the meeting. Usually you or your trustee will have approached creditors before the meeting and, where possible, will have obtained "voting letters" confirming their support.

The vote on a proposal is taken by class of creditors. Most proposals are offered to only unsecured creditors so the vote is straightforward. If another class of creditors, for example secured creditors, is addressed separately, that class must also support the proposal. If the unsecured creditors support the proposal and the secured creditors do not, the proposal cannot be enforced against the secured creditors and they will continue to have whatever rights to collection or seizure of assets existed before the filing of the proposal. In this example, assuming the company required its secured assets in order to continue operating, the result of this refusal by the secured creditors would probably be the inability of the company to go forward with its proposal, despite having the support of the unsecured creditors.

If the proposal is not approved, your business or, if it's unincorporated, you personally will be deemed to be bankrupt, and the trustee handling the proposal will automatically become trustee in the bankruptcy. The meeting of creditors on the proposal would then become the first meeting of creditors in the bankruptcy. A brief review of the process in a business bankruptcy is included in Chapter 9.

4. Obtaining Court Approval of Your Accepted Proposal

On the other hand, let's be positive! Assuming that your proposal is approved by your creditors, your trustee will proceed by filing a report with the court and by bringing the proposal to court for approval. The court review is required by the BIA to ensure that the proposal, although approved by your creditors, can be successfully completed and that it is commercially viable. As well, the court will question the nature of the financial problems of the business to confirm that they were truly the result of unfortunate circumstances, such as factors outside of your control or a mistaken operating decision, and not the result of illegal, fraudulent or reckless activities. Refusal by the court to approve the proposal will automatically result in a bankruptcy. In practice, though, since business problems seldom reflect those types of improprieties, the court's approval is withheld only in rare circumstances.

5. Fulfilling the Terms of Your Proposal

Having obtained court approval, the company or you personally will begin to fulfill the obligations as agreed in the proposal. These may involve the transfer of certain monies or other assets to the trustee, making certain payments to the trustee, issuing shares to creditors, etc.

All monies paid to or realized by your trustee in your proposal are kept in a separate trust account on behalf of your creditors. Those monies will be paid out by your trustee in accordance with the accepted and approved terms of your proposal.

Once all of your obligations under the proposal are fulfilled, your trustee will issue a certificate of full

Figure 2	**Steps in the Proposal Process**

TIMING	STEPS IN THE ORDINARY PROPOSAL
Start	Meet trustee for initial assessment. If critical, file notice of intent to make a proposal
Within five days of filing notice of intent	Trustee notifies all creditors of thirty-day stay of proceedings
Within ten days of filing notice of intent	File projected cash-flow statement and related certifications
Within thirty days of filing notice of intent	Prepare and file proposal. Trustee mails proposal to creditors with notice of meeting to vote on proposal
Within three weeks of filing proposal	Creditors' meeting. If defeated, immediate bankruptcy. If approved, continue with performance
Usually within three to four weeks of meeting approving proposal	Attend at court for approval of proposal
After court approval of proposal	Performance – agreed transfer of assets and/or payments to trustee. Performance – trustee periodically distributes payments to creditors
After debtor has completed all obligations pursuant to approved proposal	Trustee issues certificate of full performance and finalizes file

performance to your company or to you personally. At that time, you or your company will have no further obligations to your trustee or to the creditors included in the proposal on account of any balance of unpaid debt.

6. Failure of a Proposal

Having gained your creditors' support and the court's approval, it will be critical for you to fulfill the commitments as agreed. If you do not perform as agreed, a default in performance under the proposal will result in bankruptcy. This could occur if, for example, two years into a three-year payment plan, you are unable to maintain payments to the trustee. Obviously, then, meeting the obligations under the proposal will be paramount to your retaining the ability to carry on with your business.

8

—

Phoenix
Techniques

Creativity in financially restructuring a business is not
restricted to the development of a proposal to creditors.
Sometimes a failing business can be reorganized through
receivership or bankruptcy proceedings. This chapter
reviews two approaches which effectively withdraw the
life of the business in order for it to be reborn, rising from
its ashes.

1. RECEIVERSHIP FLIP

You have probably read at least one story in the news-
paper about someone whose business closed and soon
thereafter re-opened under an almost identical name. The
same person continued to run the new business, having
shed the creditors of the old business. And, as part of this
scenario, that person continued to live in the same manner

as before the business failure, apparently unaffected by it. I will explain how that came about, and you will see that you have the legal ability, subject to structuring your affairs properly, to achieve the same kind of business rebirth.

Earlier, when discussing your secured creditors' rights, I referred to the appointment of a receiver to seize and sell the secured business assets. Under provisions in a security agreement, a receiver can be appointed by your bank. If you were careful when you invested money in your business and took back security from your incorporated company, you could also be in position as a secured creditor to appoint a receiver. A receiver's responsibility is to sell the secured assets in a commercially viable manner to realize the fair market value of those assets on behalf of the secured creditor. In other words, as long as the method of sale makes sense under the circumstances, and as long as the sale price is at least equal to the fair market value of the assets, there is nothing that anyone could complain about.

So let's suppose that your business is in trouble. You can no longer afford to operate and keep up both your current expenses and bank loan obligations. As well, you cannot make payments on overdue debts. Assuming that you have an honest and forthright relationship with your banker (who probably holds security over all assets of the business), you can advise the bank of your inability to make payments and surrender the business assets to a receiver acting for the bank. Although the fair market value of the corporation's assets seized by the receiver may be less than the amount of the secured bank loan, their value might be greater to you if you could continue to use them in business. In fact, you might consider buying them for a price greater than fair market value, possibly for the amount of the bank debt. In these circumstances, if you have a good relationship with your bank, its receiver could sell the assets to you personally or to another company of yours for that greater price. In some situations the bank might lend you or your new company the money to purchase the assets from the receiver for a price equal to the bank's secured debt and thereby effectively roll over the old secured loan into the new company.

As a result of this sale, you could continue to carry on business under your name or the new company's name, with the same assets, location and staff as before. The very significant difference between your circumstances before and after the sale is the elimination of probably all debt other than the secured bank debt.

That's basically how it works.

Now, if you were wise and took back security from your own company when you invested cash in the business, you are also a secured creditor of your company. Don't forget the discussion regarding "Lending Money To Your Company" in Chapter 4. Here is how that security can be so valuable.

When you discuss your business problems with the bank and ask it to appoint a receiver to allow the sale of assets from the business to your new company, the bank may not be willing to enter that process to accommodate you. The bank may be reluctant to incur the time, costs and associated risks. It may be holding your personal guarantee and may want to stay out of any reorganization. It may simply want to be paid. On the other hand, if you loaned money to the company and hold registered valid security on the business's assets, even if your rights rank after those of the bank, you might be able to persuade the bank to allow you to appoint a receiver to control the process on your behalf. The bank would continue to hold its first charge on the same assets, even after they were sold by your receiver to a new company, so their security position will essentially remain the same. And, if you are in that rare situation in which there is no bank debt and your security ranks first over all company assets, you will definitely control the process.

I'll now explain why this is perfectly legal. If the bank's receiver (or yours) had simply sold the assets by public auction or advertised for public tenders to purchase them, the market value of those assets would have been realized by the receiver. If the proceeds were less than the amount of secured bank debt owing, the bank would have suffered a shortfall. If, however, the proceeds had exceeded the bank debt, the surplus would belong to the company's other creditors. In situations in which there would have been a shortfall, these types of flips are legal because

- the price you pay for the assets must be equal to or greater than the price obtainable in the public marketplace (a pricing that no one could criticize), and

■ there is no realistic expectation that a sale by a receiver to any arm's-length purchaser would result in a surplus for unsecured creditors (this being supported by independent appraisals of the assets being sold).

So the next time you hear about a business failing and then immediately re-opening with the same principals and continuing to operate under a new name, with no obligations to previous unsecured creditors, you're probably hearing about a "receivership flip." It's legal and can be very effective.

Before you run out to structure your receivership, you should be aware of some restricting conditions inherent in this process. In the absence of a formal proposal or bankruptcy, the priority positions of certain trusts and "deemed trusts" must be respected. For example, government claims for employee withholding taxes are a trust that must be paid in priority to all other creditors in all situations. However, GST and PST are "deemed trusts" (i.e., trusts created by a statute) that must be paid ahead of preferred and unsecured creditors in normal business situations as well as in a receivership. However, when a proposal or bankruptcy is filed, GST and PST become unsecured creditors in those proceedings and lose their priority ranking.

The effect of a proposal and bankruptcy on these priorities can be seen in the following example:

	Normal Business or Receivership	Proposal or Bankruptcy
Proceeds of Sale of Assets	$100,000	$100,000
Deduct: administrative costs	15,000	15,000
	85,000	85,000
Deduct: trust claims		
Wage withholding taxes	4,000	4,000
GST	15,000	nil
PST	12,000	nil
	31,000	4,000
	$ 54,000	$ 81,000
Amount of Secured Debt	$ 81,000	$ 81,000
Shortfall	$ 27,000	nil

You will see from the above that, in a receivership, the purchase price would have to be increased by an additional $27,000 to $127,000 in order to provide sufficient dollars to pay both the trust claims of the government and the secured debt. Even if the only payment is intended to be a secured note (i.e., a paper transaction) the sale triggers a direct liability of the secured creditor, to a maximum of the proceeds of sale, which must be paid at the time of the sale.

If the amount of these government trust liabilities is relatively small, the receivership process can make sense, since it minimizes disruption of the ongoing business.

Where the amount of receivership trust payments is material in relation to the value of the assets being purchased, the approach of a structured and planned bankruptcy and subsequent repurchase of the ongoing business may be appropriate. That process is described below.

2. STRUCTURED BANKRUPTCY FLIP

Although the filing of an assignment in bankruptcy implies the cessation and liquidation of a business's operations and the sale of its assets at distress values, there are occasions when it can be used as a step toward the reorganization and continuity of a troubled business.

You will recall that a Division I proposal requires the support of a majority of the unsecured creditors, who must also hold at least two-thirds of the total dollars of debt owed. Sometimes it is impossible to gain that level of support in negotiations. By bankrupting the business, creditors would be faced with the harsh reality of a realization based on the net proceeds of the sale of the assets in a distress situation.

In this circumstance, you would have two restructuring options available.

A bankrupt corporation or individual has the right to come out of bankruptcy by presenting a proposal to the creditors in the bankruptcy, which, if accepted by the creditors, would nullify the bankruptcy and return control of the business to the insolvent debtor. In this situation, the creditors would be comparing a determined estimate of a low realization in distress to your proposal offer (which would undoubtedly be materially more attractive). This comparison of a definite low yield on debt in bankruptcy to a probable much higher yield from the proposal could carry considerable weight in persuading the creditors to agree to your proposal. Once your creditors and the court have approved the proposal, the previous bankruptcy filing would be annulled and you would once again be in control of your renewed business.

This approach is obviously harsh and carries with it significantly more risk than the direct route to a creditor and court-approved proposal. This approach would be considered only when you expect the creditors, once confronted with the certainty of their loss in bankruptcy, would be amenable to being persuaded to accept the promise of a materially higher return (and a smaller loss) through the proposal route.

The second restructuring option to consider, after the assignment of the company into bankruptcy, is your purchase of the business assets from the trustee. The trustee's responsibility in the bankruptcy is to maximize the realization from the sale of the business assets for the general benefit of all creditors. This requires the trustee to explore all possible markets for the best and most commercially viable method of selling the assets for the highest price.

If you are certain that no other buyer exists who would be willing to pay more for the corporation's assets than you would, then you personally or another party (probably controlled directly or indirectly by you) could enter the process as a buyer of your company's assets. As long as the trustee is obtaining the best price available in the market for the assets, whether by private sale, sale by public tender or auction, it is likely that this scenario would be effective and you would ultimately have control of those assets. Your financing arrangements for this program would certainly have to be assured before contemplating going ahead with the bankruptcy filing. As mentioned earlier, this approach may sometimes provide the solution for overcoming prohibitively large GST and PST trust claim liabilities.

In both of the above scenarios, although carefully pre-structured, the filing of the bankruptcy will often require closure of the business operations during bankruptcy. Considerations that will be important to the future viability of the business, such as the possible losses of employees, customers and physical premises, the exposure of directors to trust liabilities (see below), as well as certain liabilities such as vacation pay and termination costs that follow to the successor employer, must be addressed if this course of action is contemplated.

3. DIRECTORS' LIABILITY

In all of our discussions of proposals and bankruptcies, and particularly in relation to the above phoenix techniques, one important exposure always remains – the directors' potential statutory liability for unremitted wage withholding tax, GST and PST, as well as liabilities to employees for wages and vacation pay. These are all business debts for which directors may be held personally liable. In most owner-managed businesses, the board of directors will include the owners and often their spouses or children. For this reason, in your capacity as shareholder and director, you can be liable for these obligations.

Whether this directors' liability can be defended and avoided will be a matter of the individual circumstances and arguments that can be raised by the directors. Assuming that the directors are probably responsible for these liabilities, you must always be aware of this ongoing exposure. For example, if one of the above routes is followed and the company pays all withholding tax trust claims out of a bankruptcy or proposal, the unpaid GST and PST still remain as contingent liabilities of the directors. Therefore, any planning for the company's reorganization must recognize these attendant personal exposures.

Sometimes, if the directors do not have any significant personal assets that would be exposed to these trust liabilities, personal proposals or bankruptcies filed simultaneously with the reorganization of the company could be the step necessary to settle their personal exposures. This area must be considered carefully with your trustee when reviewing your reorganization options.

9

The Self-Employed
Professional

As a self-employed professional, you know you're facing
a growing financial crisis if

- every month you're scrambling to collect accounts
  to cover your payroll and rent,
- you are often torn between paying a business debt
  and drawing cash for your personal living expenses,
- your GST and personal income tax installments are
  several months in arrears, and
- you are anxiously hoping for a new major piece of
  business to bring in a sizable retainer that can relieve
  your cash-flow problems.

Add to the above an unexpected financial crisis, such as
a substantial reassessment from Revenue Canada, and
you've lost control of your financial life.

You also know, from your own professional practice, that resolving any client problem is defined by the following steps:

(a) Your client must be helped to acknowledge and define the problem.

(b) You must outline the options available to confront and resolve the problem, including any related risks as well as the benefits of these options.

(c) A plan must be committed to and implemented.

It is very important to first acknowledge that you deserve to respect yourself as much as you do your client. And you should therefore allow yourself the same process that you apply when helping your clients.

Perhaps the most difficult issue you face derives from the differences between how you are seen by your clients and how you see yourself. By definition, as a professional, you are a problem solver and your clients, you hope, leave your office feeling good about the service you've rendered. This is the very nature of providing a professional service – an integral characteristic of your relationship to clients is that you have the expertise and experience to resolve their problems. Sometimes they may even see you as a miracle worker! They might be right.

But at the end of the day, you are facing your financial pressures alone and, unless there's a rich friend or relative around the corner who is going to bail you out, you must develop a solution yourself.

Need more money? You can work longer hours (assuming that additional business is available and the government hasn't restricted your earning ability) and hope the related work stress won't hurt you. But you can't take a vacation and give up chargeable services for even one or two weeks. And, even with those extra after-tax earnings, you will possibly still be unable to pay those additional income tax installments. The inherent dilemma in this scenario won't go away until you take your own advice and proactively restructure your financial life.

Cut back on living expenses? The challenge of this approach is to reconsider already committed expenditures such as children's tuition and camp fees. Everyone's budget includes some items that can be reduced or eliminated, but in and of themselves they may not necessarily make the difference needed.

Ultimately, resolution of your financial problems will include a number of components and will affect income, expenditures and assets retained, as well as a restructuring and possible settlement of debt. Whatever the ingredients, the goals of a successful restructuring are to

(a) regain control of your financial life,

(b) maintain your personal dignity,

(c) gain peace of mind.

Throughout this book we have considered a business as a separate entity. As an unincorporated professional, your business and you personally are intrinsically intertwined.

DEAR CREDITOR

Your personal assets and those of your unincorporated professional practice all are ultimately your assets for the purpose of presenting a proposal to creditors. A similar blending of personal and business creditors results in all creditors being joined in the proposal. This blending can be seen in the example shown as Case Study 2.

1. PURPOSE OF THE PROFESSIONAL PROPOSAL

For you as a professional (doctor, lawyer, dentist, accountant, etc.), a major goal of your proposal will be to retain your assets (within reason) and hence allow you to continue to practice and earn income. The other prime goal will be to obtain agreement from your creditors as to how much you will pay them as a settlement and when those payments will be made.

2. STRUCTURE OF THE PROFESSIONAL PROPOSAL

In order to be able to commit to any future payments to your creditors, you must be allowed to retain the assets necessary to allow you to continue to practice your profession. Often those assets are pledged as security to a financial institution. In these instances, arrangements must be made separately to compromise the debt or to continue the payments to the secured creditor and thereby retain the assets. This can usually be arranged since secured creditors normally do not want to seize your depreciated assets – they would rather continue receiving payments and realize more money as a result.

Your proposal must be seen as more beneficial to unsecured creditors than the alternative of bankruptcy. Often bankruptcy will seriously restrict or possibly end your ability to practice your profession and will result in smaller or even no payments to creditors. Because of this possible result, creditors will usually try to work with a professional to permit a meaningful proposal to be developed and accepted.

If you have previously taken appropriate steps to protect your family assets, and they are legally in your spouse's name, his or her support at this time will be a critical part of structuring your proposal to creditors. For example, a component of your proposed settlement may be a voluntary payment from your spouse, conditional on the approval of your proposal by your creditors. This certainly offers a very real element of leverage to your position, since the contribution appears only if the proposal is supported.

Sometimes a professional has accumulated some non-essential assets such as a cottage, boat or vacation condominium to which he or she has strong emotional ties. While it may be difficult contemplating their loss, you must recognize that the exercise of negotiating a proposal will require concessions from you as well as from your creditors. Selling non-essential assets to produce payments to your creditors will go a long way toward persuading them of your sincerity and commitment to start fresh and continue in control of your finances.

DEAR CREDITOR

The specific trade-offs necessary to win creditor support will vary with each person's circumstances and will also be affected by the debtor's personal relationship with his or her creditors and the history of performance under each of the debts.

3. SPECIAL CREDITORS

(a) Your Secured Creditor

It is likely that your business assets, including accounts receivable and equipment, are currently financed by a secured financial institution (e.g., bank or equipment financier). Assuming that the realizable value of the secured assets is equal to or less than the amount of related secured debt, your secured creditor will probably be pleased to continue with your existing financing arrangements. After all, once your financial reorganization under the proposal is implemented, you will be in charge of your finances once again and no longer suffering under the pressure to pay an insurmountable amount of unsecured debt. The secured lender will then anticipate that you will comfortably continue to make payments on its debt. The lender's only alternative would be to seize the secured assets, sell them at distress value and then recover some small portion of the resulting shortfall through your proposal. Full or substantial payment and continuity of their position are usually the more satisfactory benefits of supporting your proposal efforts. Therefore,

in most instances, you should find your secured creditors to be supportive and cooperative in the proposal
process. Your trustee can be extremely helpful in presenting the realities of the situation to your bank and
in securing your bank's cooperation. The weight of the
trustee's involvement will lend certainty to the bank's
decision-making process.

(b) Taxed To Debt – Revenue Canada
Enforcement of Collection

Revenue Canada has a number of enforcement tools
it can employ in the process of collecting tax debt.
Briefly, these are:

- **Demand** This can be either a phone call or letter sent after the usual series of statements and
  notices of outstanding tax obligations, setting a
  final date after which failure to pay may result in
  legal action being taken to enforce collection.

- **Requirement to Pay** The equivalent of a gar-
  nishment order from a sheriff pursuant to obtaining judgment in court, this is usually served on
  any known parties who may owe money to
  the taxpayer (e.g., bank, employer, clients). This
  requirement can demand a portion or all of the
  monies due the taxpayer and even extends to self-
  administered RRSPs.

- **Writ of Seizure** The most powerful tool available, the writ of seizure allows Revenue Canada

to send a sheriff to seize a taxpayer's personal property. In order to take this step, Revenue Canada must first present the debt to the federal court and have the debt certified to be owing. That certification is then presented to a sheriff for execution and seizure and sale of the assets.

As with all outstanding legal actions, those commenced by Revenue Canada are automatically stayed as a result of your filing either a notice of intent to make a proposal or the actual proposal.

Revenue Canada as a Party to the Proposal

Considerations regarding a Division I proposal by a professional will often lead to consideration of Revenue Canada's position as a creditor. Whether the tax debt arose from unremitted payroll or GST obligations, a reassessment of prior years' taxes or arrears from personal tax obligations (including unreported income tax liabilities), somehow Her Majesty almost always appears, in at least one or more of these forms, in the line-up of creditors.

Please take note of one important exception to the last statement. Unremitted payroll withholding taxes (income taxes, Canada Pension Plan and Employment Insurance deductions) hold a priority position ahead of other creditors when payments are made out of a proposal. Otherwise, Revenue Canada has no higher priority to distribution and has the same ranking for voting as any other unsecured creditor such as Visa or a personal loan obligation to a friend.

So, when developing your proposal, consider the government debt as simply another debt that must be addressed. If the amount is large and significant enough to affect the outcome of the vote on your proposal, you must address it and persuade Revenue Canada as you would any other large unsecured creditor. Revenue Canada's concerns will usually be similar to those of any unsecured creditor – that the offer is meaningful, achievable and results in a better return to creditors than would a bankruptcy. As well, Revenue Canada will require that the taxpayer comply with filing of all outstanding and ongoing tax returns, as well as the payment of tax installments as they become due.

Whenever possible, your trustee should present the proposal (or draft proposal) to your major creditors for their approval and support as early as possible. There is no difference between presenting that proposal to Revenue Canada and to other major creditors. You should expect the government to deal with your proposal in the same manner as would other creditors.

Figure 3	**A Comparison of the Effects of a Proposal vs. a Bankruptcy**	
	PROPOSAL	**BANKRUPTCY**
Medical Doctor		
Retention of Assets	Must arrange continuity of financing with secured creditor	Must arrange continuity of financing with secured creditor
	Unsecured assets are retained as agreed in the proposal	Unsecured assets are subject to seizure and sale by trustee; patient list may be subject to seizure and sale
		Accounts receivable from patients (including government plan payments) will be collected by trustee
Cash Flow	Cash flow continues as normal, subject to any agreed payments under proposal	Must provide for interim cash flow since accounts receivable seized by trustee for creditors
Reporting Requirements	None	None
Licence (accreditation)	No effect	No effect
Dentist		
Retention of Assets	Same as doctor	Same as doctor
Cash Flow	Same as doctor	Same as doctor
Reporting Requirements	None	None
Licence (accreditation)	Same as doctor	Same as doctor
Lawyer		
Retention of Assets	Must arrange continuity of financing with secured creditor	Must arrange continuity of financing with secured creditor
	Unsecured assets are retained as agreed in the proposal	Unsecured assets and accounts receivable are subject to seizure and sale/collection
Cash Flow	Same as doctor	Same as doctor
Reporting Requirements	None	Must report bankruptcy

	PROPOSAL	BANKRUPTCY
Licence (accreditation)	No effect	Professional designation not affected; however, unable to maintain trust account as undischarged bankrupt (usually nine months)
Chartered Accountant		
Retention of Assets	Same as lawyer	Same as lawyer
Cash Flow	Same as lawyer	Same as lawyer
Reporting Requirements		Must report bankruptcy
Licence (accreditation)	No effect	Licence suspended during bankruptcy – reinstated on application after discharge (unless reason such as fraud)

10

Bankruptcy

As indicated earlier, bankruptcy plays an important role in the restructuring process. It is ever present as the alternative result when presenting a Division I proposal to creditors. As well, certain aspects of the phoenix techniques discussed in Chapter 8 involve the formal filing of an assignment into bankruptcy.

THE PROCESS

Bankruptcy proceedings can begin through both voluntary and involuntary proceedings. The principal events that can result in bankruptcy proceedings are the following:

1. Involuntary Proceedings

(a) Petition to the court by an unsecured creditor, asking the court to confirm that the debtor is insolvent and to issue a receiving order, appointing a trustee to administer the bankruptcy

(b) Failure to perform as agreed in an approved proposal

(c) Failure to file required documents within the prescribed times (such as a cash-flow statement within ten days of filing the notice of intent to make a proposal, or a proposal within thirty days of filing the notice of intent)

(d) Refusal of the presented proposal by a vote of creditors at the meeting of creditors

(e) Refusal of the court to approve a proposal

2. Voluntary Proceedings

(a) Filing of an assignment in bankruptcy by the company or individual

In all of the above circumstances, the formal processes of bankruptcy, starting from the date of the bankruptcy event, are identical. The following chart illustrates the major steps:

Figure 4 **Steps in the Bankruptcy Process**	

Start	Voluntary – Filing of assignment in bankruptcy
	Involuntary – Court order
	         – Deemed bankruptcy on refusal
	           of proposal;
	trustee takes possession of assets of bankrupt
	company

Within five days of bankruptcy	Trustee mails notice of bankruptcy and creditors' meeting to all creditors
Before creditors' meeting	Examination of officer of company by Official Receiver
Three weeks from filing	Meeting of creditors, appointment of inspectors
Trustee administers bankrupt estate	Realization of proceeds from assets Determination of priorities for assets Disposition of assets and receipt of funds for creditors
Finalization of estate	Trustee prepares final statement of receipts and disbursements; approval by inspectors, superintendent of bankruptcy and court
Distribution of estate funds	Trustee distributes net funds (dividends) to creditors
Closure	Trustee obtains final discharge and closes file

11

Definitions

BANKRUPTCY

Bankruptcy is a legal process that results from a company or individual filing an assignment in bankruptcy or being placed into bankruptcy by a court as a result of a creditor petitioning the court for that remedy. It can also result from the refusal of creditors or the court to approve a Division I proposal (see Chapter 6). All assets of the debtor are seized and sold by a trustee appointed to wind up the affairs of the debtor and distribute the proceeds of the realization among the debtor's creditors.

DEFERRED YEAR-END

For the past several years, all unincorporated entrepreneurs have been required to maintain their tax year-ends as December 31. More than any other group, most professionals had previously employed year-ends of January 31 or February 28, allowing them to maintain a deferral of one year's income tax on a continuing basis. Rather than absorbing the full deferred year's income at once, transition rules allowed the deferred income to be recognized for tax purposes over a ten-year period.

Entrepreneurs filing a Division I proposal should, where practical, consider recognizing deferred income as current income in the tax year preceding the filing of the proposal, thus including the related deferred tax in the total debt being compromised in the proposal. This is particularly important since the exercise will result in a clean sweep of all related future tax liabilities as well as current tax liabilities up to the date of filing the notice of intent to make a proposal or the proposal itself. Revenue Canada's acceptance of this planning technique will be dependent on the circumstances of the particular proposal.

INSOLVENCY

The condition of not being able to pay bills when due. Refusal to pay bills when due can also determine insolvency when a creditor is pursuing collection in court or petitioning the court to place a debtor into bankruptcy.

Insolvency must be demonstrated in order to qualify a company or individual to file for protection under the Bankruptcy and Insolvency Act.

NOTICE OF INTENT TO ENFORCE SECURITY (filed under the Bankruptcy and Insolvency Act)

Formal notice served on a debtor by a secured creditor, confirming that a default has occurred in performance by the debtor and that the secured creditor will be exercising its rights under a security agreement to seize and sell secured assets after the expiry of a ten-day notice period.

NOTICE OF INTENT TO MAKE A PROPOSAL

Formal notice filed by a debtor, advising all creditors that a Division I proposal will be formally filed within thirty days of the filing of the notice. This notice of intent acts as a stay of proceedings against all creditors during the period from filing until the proposal has been voted on and presented to court for approval. Refusal of the filed proposal by either the creditors or the court results in automatic bankruptcy of the debtor and takes effect as of the date of the original filing (whether that was the notice of intent to make a proposal or the proposal itself).

PROPOSAL

A proposal is any offer of compromise that a debtor's creditors are willing to accept. Proposals can be informal (arranged directly between a debtor and creditors) or formal (filed under the Bankruptcy and Insolvency Act and administered by a trustee).

A consumer proposal (Division II) is an offer to creditors by an individual whose debt, excluding obligations under the principal residence's mortgage, totals less than $75,000. All other debtors, whether corporations or individuals not qualifying for a consumer proposal, can file only a Division I proposal.

REALIZABLE VALUE

In the context of insolvency proceedings (proposals and bankruptcies), the real value of your assets is often significantly lower than your perception of their value.

Equipment is normally sold at distress values, at prices obtained by a professional liquidator. That price is the amount obtainable at auction or by publicly advertising for bids. So forget what you paid for the assets or what you could privately obtain if you sold off the assets piecemeal by negotiating with many individual purchasers.

Accounts receivable will be collected in the most cost-effective and commercially viable manner available in the circumstances. The collection process could sometimes involve the principal of the insolvent debtor but is usually handled by a third-party collection agency.

When analyzing the alternative value of each asset in a distress sale, you must do so in the context of a trustee realizing on those assets.

RECEIVER

A legal person (corporation or individual) appointed as an agent for a secured creditor, for the purpose of seizing and selling the debtor's secured assets pursuant to a written and properly registered security agreement. This person is usually a trustee in bankruptcy.

STAY OF PROCEEDINGS

Effective at the moment of filing a bankruptcy, proposal or notice of intent to make a proposal, all creditors' actions against the debtor are automatically stopped or "stayed." Continuance of existing actions or the filing of a new action against the debtor can occur only by the creditor obtaining a court order allowing the legal actions to continue.

TRUSTEE IN BANKRUPTCY

Trustees in bankruptcy are licensed by the federal government and, in most cases, are chartered accountants who have specialized in the area of bankruptcy, met certain experience requirements, and have passed both written and oral exams to obtain their licenses. Trustees are actually officers of the court. Once a bankruptcy or proposal is filed, the trustee's role is to represent all creditors and to ensure that the administration is carried out in accordance with the law. This role entails ensuring that both creditors' and debtors' rights are respected in the process.

CASE STUDIES

Names used in these case studies are entirely fictitious.
Any similarity to actual persons is purely coincidental.

Case Study 1

GORDON SMITH, M.D.

History

Looking back, Gordon Smith reflected on the successful medical practice he had run for over thirty years. Both his children had graduated from university and were now established in their own careers. His modest home, partially mortgaged, and some RRSPs were evidence of his careful and responsible approach to finances and family security. Yet, during the last two years, everything was unravelling.

A six-month illness had virtually halved his income, and after paying the costs of his daughter's wedding, his cash flow was seriously strained. Having directed his reduced income to immediate needs, he had stopped making installment payments toward his income taxes, always expecting to catch up later. However, in short order, tax arrears of about $90,000 appeared on his tax bills. For a full year he tried to negotiate terms for repayment with Revenue Canada but wasn't seeing any real progress. As a result, Revenue Canada issued a requirement-to-pay notice and was garnishing 20% of his fees directly from OHIP, Ontario's health insurance plan. This only increased his cash-flow problems since he now had no money to pay his current tax obligations. His total exposure for taxes had become insurmountable.

Dr. Smith's financial position when we met is summarized on page 102.

SCHEDULE OF PERSONAL ASSETS

ASSETS	ESTIMATED REALIZABLE VALUE
One-half interest in matrimonial home	$55,000
Ontario Health Insurance Plan – receivables	6,000
Cash on hand	7,000
Personal investments	1,000
TOTAL	$69,000

LIABILITIES	
Revenue Canada	$205,000

MONTHLY STATEMENT OF FAMILY INCOME AND EXPENSES

INCOME (after tax)	$6,500
Spouse's contribution	1,500
	$8,000

EXPENSES

Mortgage	1,803
Second mortgage	600
House expenses (total)	748
Food	910
Prescription drugs	50
Clothing	300
Life insurance	718
Car insurance	180
Professional fees	450
Car operating expenses	595
Transportation to/from work (spouse)	187
Laundry/dry cleaning	50
Other expenses	500
	$7,091
Excess of income over expenses	$ 909

The Selling Document

The following is the proposal we developed with Dr. Smith. Each of the required ingredients outlined in Chapter 6 is included in the proposal.

Court File No. 31-123456

ONTARIO COURT OF JUSTICE
(GENERAL DIVISION)
IN BANKRUPTCY

In the Matter of the Proposal of
Dr. Gordon Smith
of the City of Toronto,
in the Province of Ontario

PROPOSAL

Gordon Smith, the above named debtor, hereby submits the following Proposal in accordance with the terms of the Bankruptcy and Insolvency Act (the 'BIA'):

1. THAT payment in priority to all other claims of all claims directed by the said Act to be so paid in the distribution of the property of an insolvent person shall be provided for as follows:

   (a) Claims of Her Majesty in right of Canada or a province of all amounts of a kind that could be subject to a demand under subsection 224(1.2) of the Income Tax Act or under any substantially similar provision of provincial legislation that were outstanding at the time of filing of the Proposal shall be paid in full within six months of Court Approval of the Proposal.

   (b) Preferred claims, without interest, to be paid in full in priority to all claims of ordinary creditors.

2. THAT payment of all proper fees and expenses of the Trustee under this Proposal, reasonable legal and other professional fees on and incidental to the proceedings arising out of the Proposal and in connection with the preparation and administration of this Proposal, including advice to the debtor in connection therewith, shall be paid in priority to all claims of creditors.

3. THAT provision for payment of all claims of ordinary unsecured creditors shall be made as follows:

> The debtor will make the following payments to the trustee on behalf of his unsecured creditors:
>
> (1) Upon approval of this proposal, the debtor will pay to the Trustee the sum of $7,000.00;
>
> (2) Upon approval of this proposal, the debtor's wife will pay to the Trustee the sum of $20,000.00;
>
> (3) Upon approval of this proposal, the debtor will obtain a second mortgage against his half of the equity in the matrimonial home in the amount of $55,000.00, which amount will be paid to the Trustee;
>
> (4) Upon approval of this proposal by the court, the debtor will pay monthly to the trustee the sum of $500.00 for a period of 36 months, for a total of $18,000.00.

The funds received by the trustee in the proposal, totalling approximately $100,000.00 shall be applied first to payments as required under paragraphs (1) and (2) above. All remaining funds shall be distributed pro-rata to those ordinary creditors who have proved their claims with the trustee.

The creditors shall accept these payments as payments in full of their accounts.

4. THAT the debtor shall adhere to all instalment provisions of the Income Tax Act during the course of this proposal.

5. THAT the debtor shall file all tax returns as required on time and in accordance with the Income Tax Act during the course of this proposal.

6. THAT, during the course of this proposal, the debtor shall pay any amounts due to Revenue Canada resulting from any assessments forthwith and not later than 30 days from the date of any assessment.

7. THAT failure to adhere to any of the provisions under paragraphs 4, 5 and 6 above shall be deemed to be a default under this proposal.

8. THAT Mandelbaum Spergel Inc., of the City of North York, in the Province of Ontario, shall be the Trustee of this Proposal.

9. The creditors may appoint up to five Inspectors who may have, in addition to any powers of Inspectors under the Act, the power to:

> (i) receive any notice of default in the performance of the Proposal and waive any such default, and

> (ii) approve any amendment to the Proposal without calling a meeting of creditors, where the amendment would alter the schedule for and the amounts of payments to be made by me, but would not change the total amount to be paid and

> (iii) extend the time for any payment due under this Proposal.

10. THAT all proper claims against the debtor arising with respect to goods supplied, services rendered, or other consideration given after the date of the filing of this Proposal until approval by the Ontario Court of Justice (General Division), and not otherwise dealt with pursuant to this Proposal, shall be paid in full by the debtor in the ordinary course, in priority to the claims of all other creditors.

Dated at Toronto, Ontario this 7th day of August, 1998.

Gordon Smith

To negotiate a debt compromise, a debtor must initially demonstrate that the proposal is offering creditors a better realization than they could reasonably expect if they refused the proposal and a bankruptcy ensued. Look at the offer in paragraph 3 above and compare the creditors' position in the proposal to that expected from a bankruptcy (page 106).

ASSETS	OFFERED IN PROPOSAL	EXPECTED TO REALIZE IN BANKRUPTCY
Cash on hand	$7,000	$7,000
Contribution from wife	20,000	Nil
Proceeds from mortgage	55,000	40,000 to 55,000
Total monthly payments by debtor	18,000	4,500
Possible payments as condition of discharge	Nil	Unknown
TOTAL	$100,000	$51,500 to 66,500

Clearly, the projected realization in the proposal is more attractive to a creditor than that expected from a bankruptcy.

In this instance, a mortgage commitment was obtained prior to negotiating with the creditor. By arranging this beforehand, Dr. Smith presented a forthright and committed approach to resolving his financial problems. Remember that honesty and sincerity are two of the most critical elements in a successful presentation and this upfront approach reflected those qualities.

Case Study 2
ROBERT BOND
History

As a chartered accountant and partner in a large public accounting firm, Robert had enjoyed a very successful career. His family home and vacation condo had always been held in his wife's name, and that careful planning protected the substantial equity held in those properties from possible attack by his creditors.

Robert's problems began around 1990. During the previous three years, he and a friend had invested significant funds in a start-up business that, unfortunately, did not succeed. His total investment was lost. He had also borrowed funds for this investment, and those personal loans still remained unpaid. As well, the market value of his securities portfolio diminished dramatically at the same time and he sold the equities for low realizations in a desperate chase for cash. His financial situation became critical when, during the early 1990s, the profitability of his professional practice fell dramatically and Robert was unable to cover his day-to-day living expenses.

During the past several years he had been borrowing from a number of financial institutions to assist in his investments and ongoing living expenses. Almost all of those loans were unsecured. While his investments had a high value and his personal level of earnings was substantial, Robert had little concern about his ability to pay that debt. But with the sale of his investments for cash to live on, and the reduction in his personal earnings, he soon was unable to maintain his debt payments and still have enough cash left over to cover living expenses.

His financial position when we met is summarized below.

ASSETS		ESTIMATED REALIZABLE VALUE
Cash on hand		$22,000
Vehicle 1		3,000
Vehicle 2		3,500
Interest in partnership	Value 100,000	
Less secured debt	(100,000)	Nil
Total		**$28,500**

UNSECURED LIABILITIES	
Bank 1	$133,000
Bank 2	25,000
Bank 3	24,000
Bank 4	40,000
Trust Company 1	132,000
Trust Company 2	175,000
Personal loan	24,000
Credit Card 1	1,000
Credit Card 2	500
Credit Card 3	8,500
Credit Card 4	250
Credit Card 5	1,500
Total	$564,750

MONTHLY STATEMENT OF INCOME AND EXPENSES

INCOME (after tax)	$7,500
Interest on capital	500
	$8,000
EXPENSES	
Business promotion	$500
Automobile expenses (2 cars)	1,400
Property taxes	400
Utilities	350
Food, etc.	900
Medical	50
Clothing	350
Home maintenance, insurance	200
Children's education costs	1,000
Vacation	350
Sundry	300
Debt service re: funds	
borrowed for Proposal funding	2,000
	$7,800
Excess of income over expenses	$ 200

The Selling Document

In developing the proposal to creditors, one issue was paramount – to protect Robert's professional designation. If Robert became bankrupt, his CA designation would be automatically suspended during the period of his bankruptcy (nine months), after which he would have to apply for reinstatement after discharge from bankruptcy. Had he practiced in a small firm, the only immediate effect of bankruptcy on his day-to-day ability to practice would have been a prohibition against signing reports on financial statements in his personal name while suspended. However, under the accounting firm's partnership rules, the loss of his professional designation as a result of bankruptcy would have prohibited him from continuing as a partner in the firm, resulting in his immediate loss of clients and his livelihood. A successful proposal, on the other hand, would have no effect on his license and would allow him to continue to practice as usual.

It was therefore critical to offer a significant payment to creditors as a sign of his strong intent to avoid bankruptcy and as an offer significantly greater than the realization available to creditors in a bankruptcy. The following is the proposal we developed.

Court File No. 31-246812

ONTARIO COURT OF JUSTICE
(GENERAL DIVISION)
IN BANKRUPTCY

In the Matter of the Proposal of
Robert Bond
of the City of Toronto in the Province of Ontario

PROPOSAL

Robert Bond, the above named debtor, hereby submits the following Proposal in accordance with the terms of the Bankruptcy and Insolvency Act (the 'BIA'):

1. THAT payment of the claims of secured creditors shall be made in the usual manner or as may be agreed between the debtor and secured creditors.

2. THAT payment in priority to all other claims of all claims directed by the said Act to be so paid in the distribution of the property of an insolvent person shall be provided for as follows:

   (a) Claims of Her Majesty in right of Canada or a province of all amounts of a kind that could be subject to a demand under subsection 224(1.2) of the Income Tax Act or under any substantially similar provision of provincial legislation that were outstanding at the time of filing of the Proposal shall be paid in full within six months of Court Approval of the Proposal.

(b) Preferred claims, without interest, to be paid in full in priority to all claims of ordinary creditors.

3. THAT payment of all proper fees and expenses of the Trustee under this Proposal, reasonable legal and other professional fees on and incidental to the proceedings arising out of the Proposal and in connection with the preparation and administration of this Proposal, including advice to the debtor in connection therewith, shall be paid in priority to all claims of creditors.

4. THAT provision for all claims of Ordinary unsecured creditors shall be made as follows:

> Upon approval being obtained from the creditors and the Court, the Trustee shall receive from a third party sufficient funds to allow:

(a) Payment in full of all amounts due on claims referred to in Paragraphs 2 and 3 of this Proposal;

(b) Payment in full to all Ordinary creditors having a claim less than $1,000;

(c) Payment of a dividend of twenty-one cents on the dollar to all Ordinary creditors with proved claims in excess of $1,000.

The Ordinary creditors shall accept these payments as payments in full of their accounts.

5. THAT the debtor shall adhere to all instalment provisions of the Income Tax Act during the course of this Proposal.

6. THAT the debtor shall file all tax returns as required on time and in accordance with the Income Tax Act during the course of this Proposal.

7. THAT, during the course of this Proposal, the debtor shall pay any amounts due to Revenue Canada resulting from any assessments forthwith and not later than 30 days from the date of any assessment.

8. THAT failure to adhere to any of the provisions under paragraphs 4, 5 and 6 above shall be deemed to be a default under this Proposal.

9. THAT Mandelbaum Spergel Inc., of the City of North York, in the Province of Ontario, shall be the Trustee of this Proposal.

10. THAT the creditors may appoint up to five Inspectors who may have, in addition to any powers of Inspectors under the Act, the power to:

(i) receive any notice of default in the performance of the Proposal and waive any such default, and

(ii) approve any amendment to the Proposal without calling a meeting of creditors, where the amendment would alter the schedule for and the amounts of payments to be made by me, but would not change the total amount to be paid and

(iii) extend the time for any payment due under this Proposal.

11. THAT all proper claims against the debtor arising with respect to goods supplied, services rendered, or other consideration given after the date of the filing of the Proposal, up to the date of approval of this Proposal by the Ontario Court of Justice (General Division), and not otherwise dealt with pursuant to this Proposal, shall be paid in full by the debtor in the ordinary course, in priority to the claims of all other creditors.

Dated at Toronto, Ontario this 5th day of March, 1998.

Robert Bond

The actual payments that were made to creditors under the terms of the proposal totaled more than $100,000. You can clearly see that, had the creditors refused the proposal and forced Bond into bankruptcy, his assets (as shown above) would probably have yielded a net distribution to creditors (after administration costs) of about $20,000. As a result of prudent planning, the Bond family's principal assets had all been legally protected, in his wife's name, from his personal creditors.

In this instance, Bond was able to offer a significantly better alternative to his creditors than that available to them had he been forced into bankruptcy.

Case Study 3

XY COMPUTER SERVICES INC.

History

This company provided service under maintenance contracts for several computer clone manufacturers. Overhead
costs had risen over a period of years, and the company,
although marginally profitable, was increasingly unable to
keep up with its trade payable obligations. Operating on
a COD basis was becoming difficult, if not impossible, and
the owner, Jordan White, wished to sell or wind up the
business while there was still an element of goodwill in
the continuing operation.

The following summarizes the financial condition of the
company when we met:

ASSETS	BOOK VALUE	DISTRESS REALIZATION VALUE
Cash	$64,000	$64,000
Accounts Receivable	319,000	200,000
Sundry Receivables and Prepaid Expenses	16,000	5,000
Inventories	64,000	40,000
Equipment, furniture	54,000	10,000
Total	**$517,000**	**$319,000**

LIABILITIES	
Government Trust Claims	$60,000
Trade Accounts Payable	540,000
Accrued Liabilities	52,000
Secured Creditor (shareholder)	6,600,000
Total	**$7,252,000**

The company and its secured debt had been purchased by Jordan from its U.S. parent a number of years ago. Jordan had run the business successfully; however, the old service contracts were now expiring and there were fewer and fewer renewals. New markets had not been established and, as a result, the future of the business as a stand-alone operation was definitely in danger.

A decision was made to offer the creditors payments over three years, the total of which would be about 50% of their debt. At the same time, it was felt that there might be a market for the goodwill value of the customer base still in place and that an effort should be made to find a buyer.

Ultimately a buyer was found, Global Technology Inc., a large public company that was acquiring market share by buying up small operations like XY. Since the company had significant tax losses carried forward, Jordan could justify a price for his shares and, at the same time, expedite a settlement with creditors by making the proposal payment up front. (Remember what we said about the attraction of an up-front payment in winning creditor support for a proposal.)

Here is the proposal that was eventually filed and accepted by creditors:

Court File No. 31-777123

ONTARIO COURT OF JUSTICE
(GENERAL DIVISION)
IN BANKRUPTCY

In the Matter of the Proposal of
XY COMPUTER SERVICES INC.
A company duly incorporated under the laws of the Province of Ontario and
having its head office in the Town of Markham in the
Regional Municipality of York
In the Province of Ontario

PROPOSAL

XY Computer Services Inc., the above named debtor, hereby submits the following Proposal in accordance with the terms of the Bankruptcy and Insolvency Act (the 'BIA'):

1. THAT payment of the claims of secured creditors shall be made in the following manner:

   The secured creditor has agreed to allow this proposal to go forward and, if approved by the creditors, to not take steps to realize on its security.

2. THAT payment in priority to all other claims of all claims directed by the said Act to be so paid in the distribution of the property of an insolvent person shall be provided for as follows:

   (a) Claims of Her Majesty in right of Canada or a province of all amounts of a kind that could be subject to a demand under subsection 224(1.2) of the Income Tax Act or under any substantially similar provision of provincial legislation that were outstanding at the time of filing of the Proposal shall be paid in full within six months of Court Approval of the Proposal.

   (b) Preferred claims, without interest, to be paid in full in priority to all claims of ordinary creditors.

DEAR CREDITOR

3. THAT payment of all proper fees and expenses of the Trustee under this Proposal, reasonable legal and other professional fees on and incidental to the proceedings arising out of the Proposal and in connection with the preparation and administration of this proposal, including advice to the debtor in connection therewith, shall be paid in priority to all claims of creditors.

4. THAT provision for all claims of ordinary unsecured creditors shall be made as follows:

   The Company shall pay to the Trustee, on or before April 30, 1998, sufficient monies to allow the Trustee to make the following payments to Ordinary creditors:

   (1) To those creditors with proved claims of, or less than, $250, the full amount of their claims;

   (2) To those creditors with proved claims in excess of $250, 50% of their claims or $250, whichever amount is the greater.

   The creditors shall accept these payments as payments in full of their accounts.

5. THAT this Proposal is conditional on, prior to the Statutory Meeting of Creditors to be held to consider this Proposal, the shareholder of the Company entering into a definitive Agreement of Purchase and Sale with Global Technology Inc. for the sale of XY Computer Services Inc., one term of said agreement to be the funding of this Proposal by payment to the Trustee of the monies referred to above on or before April 30, 1998.

6. THAT Mandelbaum Spergel Inc., of the City of North York, in the Province of Ontario, shall be the Trustee of this Proposal.

7. The creditors may appoint up to five Inspectors who may have, in addition to any powers of Inspectors under the Act, the power to:

   (i) receive any notice of default in the performance of the Proposal and waive any such default, and

   (ii) approve any amendment to the Proposal without calling a meeting of creditors, where the amendment would alter the schedule for and the amounts of payments to be made by me, but would not change the total amount to be paid and

116

(iii) extend the time for any payment due under this Proposal.

8. THAT all proper claims against the debtor arising with respect to goods supplied, services rendered, or other consideration given after the date of the filing of the Proposal, up to the date of approval of this Proposal by the Ontario Court of Justice (General Division), and not otherwise dealt with pursuant to this Proposal, shall be paid in full by the debtor in the ordinary course, in priority to the claims of all other creditors.

Dated at Toronto, Ontario this 25th day of March, 1998.

_____

XY Computer Services Inc.

The success of this proposal was particularly satisfying. In his position as the secured creditor able to control all assets in the company, Jordan could have appointed a receiver to sell the assets and goodwill on his own account, leaving nothing for the unsecured creditors. As a result of the offered proposal, the unsecured creditors received immediate payment of 50 cents on the dollar and Jordan was able to personally obtain some value for the shares of the company, a value not obtainable by the creditors in any circumstance. As well, Global Technology Inc. gained another portfolio of service customers to whom it planned to market both the existing and new services. The result was a deal that maximized value for the unsecured creditors, the shareholder (and secured creditor) and the purchaser.

APPENDIX

The Bankruptcy and Insolvency Act
Part III
Division I
Proposals

NOTE TO READER

The following material has been reproduced from the Bankruptcy and Insolvency Act (Canada). Although the material includes references to other parts of the Act, it is included here only as a general source of information for the reader.

Who may make a proposal

50. (1) Subject to subsection (1.1), a proposal may be made by

(a) an insolvent person;

(b) a receiver, within the meaning of subsection 243(2), but only in relation to an insolvent person;

(c) a liquidator of an insolvent person's property;

(d) a bankrupt; and

(e) a trustee of the estate of a bankrupt.

Where proposal may not be made

(1.1) A proposal may not be made under this Division with respect to a debtor in respect of whom a consumer proposal has been filed under Division II until the administrator under the consumer proposal has been discharged.

To whom proposal made

(1.2) A proposal must be made to the creditors generally, either as a mass or separated into classes as provided in the proposal, and may also be made to secured creditors in respect of any class or classes of secured claim, subject to subsection (1.3).

Idem

(1.3) Where a proposal is made to one or more secured creditors in respect of secured claims of a particular class, the proposal must be made to all secured creditors in respect of secured claims of that class.

Classes of secured claims

(1.4) Secured claims may be included in the same class if the interests of the creditors holding those claims are sufficiently similar to give them a commonality of interest, taking into account

(a) the nature of the debts giving rise to the claims;

(b) the nature and priority of the security in respect of the claims;

(c) the remedies available to the creditors in the absence of the proposal, and the extent to which the creditors would recover their claims by exercising those remedies;

(d) the treatment of the claims under the proposal, and the extent to which the claims would be paid under the proposal; and

(e) such further criteria, consistent with those set out in paragraphs (a) to (d), as are prescribed.

Court may determine classes

(1.5) The court may, on application made at any time after a notice of intention or a proposal is filed, determine, in accordance with subsection (1.4), the classes of secured claims appropriate to a proposal, and the class into which any particular secured claim falls.

Creditors' response

(1.6) Subject to section 50.1 as regards included secured creditors, any creditor may respond to the proposal as made to the creditors generally, by filing with the trustee a proof of claim in the manner provided for in

(a) sections 124 to 126, in the case of unsecured creditors; or

(b) sections 124 to 134, in the case of secured creditors.

Effect of filing proof of claim

(1.7) Hereinafter in this Division, a reference to an unsecured creditor shall be deemed to include a secured creditor who has filed a proof of claim under subsection (1.6), and a reference to an unsecured claim shall be deemed to include that secured creditor's claim.

Voting

(1.8) All questions relating to a proposal, except the question of accepting or refusing the proposal, shall be decided by ordinary resolution of the creditors to whom the proposal was made.

Documents to be lodged

(2) Subject to section 50.4, proceedings for a proposal shall be commenced in the case of an insolvent person by lodging

with a licensed trustee, and in the case of a bankrupt by lodging with the trustee of the estate, a copy of the proposal in writing setting out the terms of the proposal and the particulars of any securities or sureties proposed, signed by the person making the proposal and the proposed sureties if any, and

(a) if the person in respect of whom the proposal is made is bankrupt, the statement of affairs referred to in section 158; or
(b) if the person in respect of whom the proposal is made is not bankrupt, a statement showing the financial position of the person at the date of the proposal, verified by affidavit as being correct to the belief and knowledge of the person making the proposal.

Approval of inspectors
(3) A proposal made in respect of a bankrupt shall be approved by the inspectors before any further action is taken thereon.

Proposal, etc., not to be withdrawn
(4) No proposal or any security or guarantee tendered therewith may be withdrawn pending the decision of the creditors and the court.

Assignment not prevented
(4.1) Subsection (4) shall not be construed as preventing an insolvent person in respect of whom a proposal has been made from subsequently making an assignment.

Duties of trustee

(5) The trustee shall make or cause to be made such an appraisal and investigation of the affairs and property of the debtor as to enable the trustee to estimate with reasonable accuracy the financial situation of the debtor and the cause of the debtor's financial difficulties or insolvency and report the result thereof to the meeting of the creditors.

Trustee to file cash-flow statement

(6) The trustee shall, when filing a proposal under subsection 62(1) in respect of an insolvent person, file with the proposal

(a) a statement indicating the projected cash-flow of the insolvent person (in this section referred to as the "cash-flow statement"), or a revised cash-flow statement where a cash-flow statement had previously been filed under subsection 50.4(2) in respect of that insolvent person, prepared by the person making the proposal, reviewed for its reasonableness by the trustee and signed by the trustee and the person making the proposal;

(b) a report on the reasonableness of the cash-flow statement, in the prescribed form, prepared and signed by the trustee; and

(c) a report containing prescribed representations by the person making the proposal regarding the preparation of the cash-flow statement, in the prescribed form, prepared and signed by the person making the proposal.

Creditors may obtain statement

(7) Subject to subsection (8), any creditor may obtain a copy of the cash-flow statement on request made to the trustee.

Exception

(8) The court may order that a cash-flow statement or any part thereof not be released to some or all of the creditors pursuant to subsection (7) where it is satisfied that

(a) such release would unduly prejudice the insolvent person; and

(b) non-release would not unduly prejudice the creditor or creditors in question.

Trustee protected

(9) If the trustee acts in good faith and takes reasonable care in reviewing the cash-flow statement, he is not liable for loss or damage to any person resulting from that person's reliance on the cash-flow statement.

Trustee to monitor and report

(10) Subject to any direction of the court under paragraph 47.1(2)(a), the trustee under a proposal in respect of an insolvent person shall, for the purpose of monitoring the insolvent person's business and financial affairs, have access to and examine the insolvent person's property, including his premises, books, records and other financial documents, to the extent necessary to adequately assess the insolvent person's

business and financial affairs, from the filing of the proposal
until the proposal is approved by the court or the insolvent
person becomes bankrupt, and shall

(a) file a report on the state of the insolvent person's business
and financial affairs, containing any prescribed information,

    (i) with the official receiver forthwith after ascertaining
any material adverse change in the insolvent person's
projected cash-flow or financial circumstances, and

    (ii) with the court at such other times as the court may
order; and

(b) send a report on the state of the insolvent person's business and financial affairs, containing any prescribed information, to the creditors and the official receiver, in the
prescribed manner, at least ten days before the meeting of
creditors referred to in subsection 51(1).

Report to creditors

(11) An interim receiver who has been directed under subsection 47.1(2) to carry out the duties set out in subsection
(10) in substitution for the trustee shall deliver a report on the
state of the insolvent person's business and financial affairs,
containing any prescribed information, to the trustee at least
fifteen days before the meeting of creditors referred to in
subsection 51(1), and the trustee shall send the report to the
creditors and the official receiver, in the prescribed manner,
at least ten days before the meeting of creditors referred to
in that subsection.

Court may declare proposal as deemed refused by creditors

(12) The court may, on application by the trustee, the interim receiver, if any, appointed under section 47.1 or a creditor, at any time before the meeting of creditors, declare that the proposal is deemed to have been refused by the creditors if the court is satisfied that

(a) the debtor has not acted, or is not acting, in good faith and with due diligence;

(b) the proposal will not likely be accepted by the creditors; or

(c) the creditors as a whole would be materially prejudiced if the application under this subsection is rejected.

Claims against directors – compromise

(13) A proposal made in respect of a corporation may include in its terms provision for the compromise of claims against directors of the corporation that arose before the commencement of proceedings under this Act and that relate to the obligations of the corporation where the directors are by law liable in their capacity as directors for the payment of such obligations.

Exception

(14) A provision for the compromise of claims against directors may not include claims that

(a) relate to contractual rights of one or more creditors arising from contracts with one or more directors; or

(b) are based on allegations of misrepresentation made by directors to creditors or of wrongful or oppressive conduct by directors.

Powers of court

(15) The court may declare that a claim against directors shall not be compromised if it is satisfied that the compromise would not be just and equitable in the circumstances.

Application of other provisions

(16) Subsection 62(2) and section 122 apply, with such modifications as the circumstances require, in respect of claims against directors compromised under a proposal of a debtor corporation.

Determination of classes of claims

(17) The court, on application made at any time after a proposal is filed, may determine the classes of claims of claimants against directors and the class into which any particular claimant's claim falls.

Resignation or removal of directors

(18) Where all of the directors have resigned or have been removed by the shareholders without replacement, any person who manages or supervises the management of the business and affairs of the corporation shall be deemed to be a director for the purposes of this section.

Secured creditor may file proof of secured claim

50.1 (1) Subject to subsections (2) to (4), a secured creditor to whom a proposal has been made in respect of a particular secured claim may respond to the proposal by filing with the trustee a proof of secured claim in the prescribed form, and may vote, on all questions relating to the proposal, in respect of that entire claim, and sections 124 to 126 apply, in so far as they are applicable, with such modifications as the circumstances require, to proofs of secured claim.

Proposed assessed value

(2) Where a proposal made to a secured creditor in respect of a claim includes a proposed assessed value of the security in respect of the claim, the secured creditor may file with the trustee a proof of secured claim in the prescribed form, and may vote as a secured creditor on all questions relating to the proposal in respect of an amount equal to the lesser of

(a) the amount of the claim, and
(b) the proposed assessed value of the security.

Idem

(3) Where the proposed assessed value is less than the amount of the secured creditor's claim, the secured creditor may file with the trustee a proof of claim in the prescribed form, and may vote as an unsecured creditor on all questions relating to the proposal in respect of an amount equal to the difference between the amount of the claim and the proposed assessed value.

Idem

(4) Where a secured creditor is dissatisfied with the proposed assessed value of his security, the secured creditor may apply to the court, within fifteen days after the proposal is sent to the creditors, to have the proposed assessed value revised, and the court may revise the proposed assessed value, in which case the revised value henceforth applies for the purposes of this Part.

Where no secured creditor in a class takes action

(5) Where no secured creditor having a secured claim of a particular class files a proof of secured claim at or before the meeting of creditors, the secured creditors having claims of that class shall be deemed to have voted for the refusal of the proposal.

Excluded secured creditor

50.2 A secured creditor to whom a proposal has not been made in respect of a particular secured claim may not file a proof of secured claim in respect of that claim.

Rights in bankruptcy

50.3 On the bankruptcy of an insolvent person who made a proposal to one or more secured creditors in respect of secured claims, any proof of secured claim filed pursuant to section 50.1 ceases to be valid or effective, and sections 112 and 127 to 134 apply in respect of a proof of claim filed by any secured creditor in the bankruptcy.

Notice of intention

50.4 (1) Before lodging a copy of a proposal with a licensed trustee, an insolvent person may file a notice of intention, in the prescribed form, with the official receiver in the insolvent person's locality, stating

(a) the insolvent person's intention to make a proposal,

(b) the name and address of the licensed trustee who has consented, in writing, to act as the trustee under the proposal, and

(c) the names of the creditors with claims amounting to two hundred and fifty dollars or more and the amounts of their claims as known or shown by the debtor's books, and attaching thereto a copy of the consent referred to in paragraph (b).

Certain things to be filed

(2) Within ten days after filing a notice of intention under subsection (1), the insolvent person shall file with the official receiver

(a) a statement indicating the projected cash-flow of the insolvent person (in this section referred to as the "cash-flow statement"), prepared by the insolvent person, reviewed for its reasonableness by the trustee under the notice of intention, and signed by the trustee and the insolvent person;

(b) a report on the reasonableness of the cash-flow statement, in the prescribed form, prepared and signed by the trustee; and

(c) a report containing prescribed representations by the insolvent person regarding the preparation of the cash-flow statement, in the prescribed form, prepared and signed by the insolvent person.

Creditors may obtain statement

(3) Subject to subsection (4), any creditor may obtain a copy of the cash-flow statement on request made to the trustee.

Exception

(4) The court may order that a cash-flow statement or any part thereof not be released to some or all of the creditors pursuant to subsection (3) where it is satisfied that

(a) such release would unduly prejudice the insolvent person; and

(b) non-release would not unduly prejudice the creditor or creditors in question.

Trustee protected

(5) If the trustee acts in good faith and takes reasonable care in reviewing the cash-flow statement, the trustee is not liable for loss or damage to any person resulting from that person's reliance on the cash-flow statement.

Trustee to notify creditors

(6) Within five days after the filing of a notice of intention under subsection (1), the trustee named therein shall send to every known creditor, in the prescribed manner, a copy thereof.

Trustee to monitor and report

(7) Subject to any direction of the court under paragraph 47.1(2)(a), the trustee under a notice of intention in respect of an insolvent person

(a) shall, for the purpose of monitoring the insolvent person's business and financial affairs, have access to and examine the insolvent person's property, including his premises, books, records and other financial documents, to the extent necessary to adequately assess the insolvent person's business and financial affairs, from the filing of the notice of intention until a proposal is filed or the insolvent person becomes bankrupt; and

(b) shall file a report on the state of the insolvent person's business and financial affairs, containing any prescribed information,

(i) with the official receiver forthwith after ascertaining any material adverse change in the insolvent person's projected cash-flow or financial circumstances, and

(ii) with the court at or before the hearing by the court of any application under subsection (9) and at such other times as the court may order.

Where assignment deemed to have been made

(8) Where an insolvent person fails to comply with subsection (2), or where the trustee fails to file a proposal with the official receiver under subsection 62(1) within a period of thirty days after the day the notice of intention was filed

under subsection (1), or within any extension of that period
granted under subsection (9),

(a) the insolvent person is, on the expiration of that period or
that extension, as the case may be, deemed to have thereupon
made an assignment;
(b) the trustee shall forthwith file a report thereof in the
prescribed form with the official receiver, who shall thereupon
issue a certificate of assignment in the prescribed form,
which has the same effect for the purposes of this Act as an
assignment filed pursuant to section 49; and
(c) the trustee shall, within five days after the day the
certificate mentioned in paragraph (b) is issued, send notice
of the meeting of creditors under section 102, at which meeting the creditors may by ordinary resolution, notwithstanding
section 14, affirm the appointment of the trustee or appoint
another licensed trustee in lieu of that trustee.

Extension of time for filing proposal
(9) The insolvent person may, before the expiration of the
thirty day period mentioned in subsection (8) or any extension
thereof granted under this subsection, apply to the court for
an extension, or further extension, as the case may be, of
that period, and the court may grant such extensions, not
exceeding forty-five days for any individual extension and not
exceeding in the aggregate five months after the expiration of
the thirty day period mentioned in subsection (8), if satisfied
on each application that

(a) the insolvent person has acted, and is acting, in good faith and with due diligence;

(b) the insolvent person would likely be able to make a viable proposal if the extension being applied for were granted; and

(c) no creditor would be materially prejudiced if the extension being applied for were granted.

Court may not extend time

(10) Subsection 187(11) does not apply in respect of time limitations imposed by subsection (9).

Court may terminate period for making proposal

(11) The court may, on application by the trustee, the interim receiver, if any, appointed under section 47.1, or a creditor, declare terminated, before its actual expiration, the thirty day period mentioned in subsection (8) or any extension thereof granted under subsection (9) if the court is satisfied that

(a) the insolvent person has not acted, or is not acting, in good faith and with due diligence,

(b) the insolvent person will not likely be able to make a viable proposal before the expiration of the period in question,

(c) the insolvent person will not likely be able to make a proposal, before the expiration of the period in question, that will be accepted by the creditors, or

(d) the creditors as a whole would be materially prejudiced were the application under this subsection rejected, and where the court declares the period in question terminated, paragraphs (8)(a) to (c) thereupon apply as if that period had expired.

Trustee to help prepare proposal

50.5 The trustee under a notice of intention shall, between the filing of the notice of intention and the filing of a proposal, advise on and participate in the preparation of the proposal, including negotiations thereon.

Calling of meeting of creditors

51. (1) The trustee shall call a meeting of the creditors, to be held within twenty-one days after the filing of the proposal with the official receiver under subsection 62(1), by sending in the prescribed manner to every known creditor and to the official receiver, at least ten days before the meeting,

(a) a notice of the date, time and place of the meeting;

(b) a condensed statement of the assets and liabilities;

(c) a list of the creditors with claims amounting to two hundred and fifty dollars or more and the amounts of their claims as known or shown by the debtor's books;

(d) a copy of the proposal;

(e) the prescribed forms, in blank, of
    (i)   proof of claim,
    (ii) in the case of a secured creditor to whom the proposal was made, proof of secured claim, and
    (iii) proxy, if not already sent; and

(f) a voting letter as prescribed.

In case of a prior meeting

(2) Where a meeting of his creditors at which a statement or list of the debtor's assets, liabilities and creditors was presented was held before the trustee is required by this section to convene a meeting to consider the proposal and at the time when the debtor requires the convening of the meeting the condition of the debtor's estate remains substantially the same as at the time of the former meeting, the trustee may omit observance of the provisions of paragraphs (1)(b) and (c).

Chairman of first meeting

(3) The official receiver, or the nominee thereof, shall be the chairman of the meeting referred to in subsection (1) and shall decide any questions or disputes arising at the meeting, and any creditor may appeal any such decision to the court.

Adjournment of meeting for further investigation and examination

52. Where the creditors by ordinary resolution at the meeting at which a proposal is being considered so require, the meeting shall be adjourned to such time and place as may be fixed by the chairman

(a) to enable a further appraisal and investigation of the affairs and property of the debtor to be made; or
(b) for the examination under oath of the debtor or of such other person as may be believed to have knowledge of the affairs or property of the debtor, and the testimony of the

debtor or such other person, if transcribed, shall be placed before the adjourned meeting or may be read in court on the application for the approval of the proposal.

Creditor may assent or dissent

53. Any creditor who has proved a claim, whether secured or unsecured, may indicate assent to or dissent from the proposal in the prescribed manner to the trustee prior to the meeting, and any assent or dissent, if received by the trustee at or prior to the meeting, has effect as if the creditor had been present and had voted at the meeting.

Vote on proposal by creditors

54. (1) The creditors may, in accordance with this section, resolve to accept or may refuse the proposal as made or as altered at the meeting or any adjournment thereof.

Voting system

(2) For the purpose of subsection (1),

(a) the following creditors with proven claims are entitled to vote:
    (i) all unsecured creditors, and
    (ii) those secured creditors in respect of whose secured claims the proposal was made;
(b) the creditors shall vote by class, according to the class of their respective claims, and for that purpose
    (i) all unsecured claims constitute one class, unless the

proposal provides for more than one class of unsecured claim, and

(ii) the classes of secured claims shall be determined as provided by subsection 50(1.4);

(c) the votes of the secured creditors do not count for the purpose of this section, but are relevant only for the purpose of subsection 62(2); and

(d) the proposal shall be deemed to be accepted by the creditors if, and only if, all classes of unsecured creditors vote for the acceptance of the proposal by a majority in number and two thirds in value of the unsecured creditors of each class present, personally or by proxy, at the meeting and voting on the resolution.

Idem

(2.1) For greater certainty, subsection 224(1.2) of the Income Tax Act shall not be construed as classifying as secured claims, for the purpose of subsection (2), claims of Her Majesty in right of Canada or a province for amounts that could be subject to a demand under subsection 224(1.2) of the Income Tax Act or under any substantially similar provision of provincial legislation.

Where no quorum in a class

(2.2) Where there is no quorum of secured creditors in respect of a particular class of secured claims, the secured creditors having claims of that class shall be deemed to have voted for the refusal of the proposal.

Related creditor

(3) A creditor who is related to the debtor may vote against but not for the acceptance of the proposal.

Voting by trustee

(4) The trustee, as a creditor, may not vote on the proposal.

Creditors may provide for supervision of debtor's affairs

55. At a meeting to consider a proposal, the creditors, with the consent of the debtor, may include such provisions or terms in the proposal with respect to the supervision of the affairs of the debtor as they may deem advisable.

Appointment of inspectors

56. The creditors may appoint one or more, but not exceeding five, inspectors of the estate of the debtor, who shall have the powers of an inspector under this Act, subject to any extension or restriction of those powers by the terms of the proposal.

Result of refusal of proposal

57. Where the creditors refuse a proposal in respect of an insolvent person,

(a) the insolvent person is deemed to have thereupon made an assignment;
(b) the trustee shall forthwith file a report thereof in the prescribed form with the official receiver, who shall thereupon

issue a certificate of assignment in the prescribed form, which has the same effect for the purposes of this Act as an assignment filed pursuant to section 49; and

(c) the trustee shall either

(i) forthwith call a meeting of creditors present at that time, which meeting shall be deemed to be a meeting called under section 102, or

(ii) if no quorum exists for the purpose of subparagraph (i), send notice, within five days after the day the certificate mentioned in paragraph (b) is issued, of the meeting of creditors under section 102,

and at either meeting the creditors may by ordinary resolution, notwithstanding section 14, affirm the appointment of the trustee or appoint another licensed trustee in lieu of that trustee.

Appointment of new trustee

57.1 Where a declaration has been made under subsection 50(12) or 50.4(11), the court may, if it is satisfied that it would be in the best interests of the creditors to do so, appoint a trustee in lieu of the trustee appointed under the notice of intention or proposal that was filed.

Application for court approval

58. On acceptance of a proposal by the creditors, the trustee shall

(a) within five days after the acceptance, apply to the court for an appointment for a hearing of the application for the court's approval of the proposal;

(b) send a notice of the hearing of the application, in the prescribed manner and at least fifteen days before the date of the hearing, to the debtor, to every creditor who has proved a claim, whether secured or unsecured, to the person making the proposal and to the official receiver;

(c) forward a copy of the report referred to in paragraph (d) to the official receiver at least ten days before the date of the hearing; and

(d) at least two days before the date of the hearing, file with the court, in the prescribed form, a report on the proposal.

Court to hear report of trustee, etc.

59. (1) The court shall, before approving the proposal, hear a report of the trustee in the prescribed form respecting the terms thereof and the conduct of the debtor, and, in addition, shall hear the trustee, the debtor, the person making the proposal, any opposing, objecting or dissenting creditor and such further evidence as the court may require.

Court may refuse to approve the proposal

(2) Where the court is of the opinion that the terms of the proposal are not reasonable or are not calculated to benefit the general body of creditors, the court shall refuse to approve the proposal, and the court may refuse to approve the proposal whenever it is established that the debtor has committed any one of the offences mentioned in sections 198 to 200.

Reasonable security

(3) Where any of the facts mentioned in section 173 or 177 are proved against the debtor, the court shall refuse to approve the proposal unless it provides reasonable security for the payment of not less than fifty cents on the dollar on all the unsecured claims provable against the debtor's estate or such percentage thereof as the court may direct.

Priority of claims

60. (1) No proposal shall be approved by the court that does not provide for the payment in priority to other claims of all claims directed to be so paid in the distribution of the property of a debtor and for the payment of all proper fees and expenses of the trustee on and incidental to the proceedings arising out of the proposal or in the bankruptcy.

Certain Crown claims

(1.1) Unless Her Majesty consents, no proposal shall be approved by the court that does not provide for the payment in full to Her Majesty in right of Canada or a province, within six months after court approval of the proposal, of all amounts of a kind that could be subject to a demand under subsection 224(1.2) of the Income Tax Act or under any substantially similar provision of provincial legislation and that were outstanding at the time of the filing

(a) of the notice of intention; or

(b) of the proposal, if no notice of intention was filed.

Idem

(1.2) No proposal shall be approved by the court if, at the time the court hears the application for approval, Her Majesty in right of Canada or a province satisfies the court that the debtor is in default on any remittance of an amount referred to in subsection (1.1) that became due after the filing

(a) of the notice of intention; or

(b) of the proposal, if no notice of intention was filed.

Proposals by employers

(1.3) No proposal in respect of an employer shall be approved by the court unless

(a) it provides for payment to the employees and former employees, immediately after court approval of the proposal, of amounts equal to the amounts that they would be qualified to receive under paragraph 136(1)(d) if the employer became bankrupt on the date of the filing of the notice of intention, or proposal if no notice of intention was filed, as well as wages, salaries, commissions or compensation for services rendered after that date and before the court approval of the proposal, together with, in the case of travelling salesmen, disbursements properly incurred by those salesmen in and about the bankrupt's business during the same period; and

(b) the court is satisfied that the employer can and will make the payments as required under paragraph (a).

Voting on proposal

(1.4) For the purpose of voting on any question relating to a proposal in respect of an employer, no person has a claim for an amount referred to in paragraph (1.3)(a).

Payment to trustee

(2) All moneys payable under the proposal shall be paid to the trustee and, after payment of all proper fees and expenses mentioned in subsection (1), shall be distributed by him to the creditors.

Distribution of promissory notes, stock, etc., of debtor

(3) Where the proposal provides for the distribution of property in the nature of promissory notes or other evidence of obligations by or on behalf of the debtor or, when the debtor is a corporation, shares in the capital stock of the corporation, the property shall be dealt with in the manner prescribed in subsection (2) as nearly as may be.

Section 147 applies

(4) Section 147 applies to all distributions made to the creditors by the trustee pursuant to subsection (2) or (3).

Power of court

(5) Subject to subsections (1) to (1.5), the court may either approve or refuse to approve the proposal.

Annulment of bankruptcy

61. (1) The approval by the court of a proposal made after bankruptcy operates to annul the bankruptcy and to revest in the debtor, or in such other person as the court may approve, all the right, title and interest of the trustee in the property of the debtor, unless the terms of the proposal otherwise provide.

Non-approval of proposal by court

(2) Where the court refuses to approve a proposal in respect of an insolvent person a copy of which has been filed under section 62,

(a) the insolvent person is deemed to have thereupon made an assignment;

(b) the trustee shall forthwith file a report thereof in the prescribed form with the official receiver, who shall thereupon issue a certificate of assignment in the prescribed form, which has the same effect for the purposes of this Act as an assignment filed pursuant to section 49; and

(c) the trustee shall, within five days after the day the certificate mentioned in paragraph (b) is issued, send notice of the meeting of creditors under section 102, at which meeting the creditors may by ordinary resolution, notwithstanding section 14, affirm the appointment of the trustee or appoint another licensed trustee in lieu of that trustee.

Costs when proposal refused

(4) No costs incurred by a debtor on or incidental to an

application to approve a proposal, other than the costs incurred by the trustee, shall be allowed out of the estate of the debtor if the court refuses to approve the proposal.

Filing of proposal

62. (1) Where a proposal is made in respect of an insolvent person, the trustee shall file a copy thereof with the official receiver.

Determination of claims

(1.1) Except in respect of claims referred to in subsection 14.06(8), where a proposal is made in respect of an insolvent person, the time with respect to which the claims of creditors shall be determined is the time of the filing of

(a) the notice of intention; or
(b) the proposal, if no notice of intention was filed.

Determination of claims re bankrupt

(1.2) Except in respect of claims referred to in subsection 14.06(8), where a proposal is made in respect of a bankrupt, the time with respect to which the claims of creditors shall be determined is the date on which the bankrupt became bankrupt.

On whom approval binding

(2) A proposal accepted by the creditors and approved by the court is binding on creditors in respect of

(a) all unsecured claims, and

(b) the secured claims in respect of which the proposal was made and that were in classes in which the secured creditors voted for the acceptance of the proposal by a majority in number and two thirds in value of the secured creditors present, personally or by proxy, at the meeting and voting on the resolution to accept the proposal, but does not release the insolvent person from the debts and liabilities referred to in section 178, unless the creditor assents thereto.

Certain persons not released

(3) The acceptance of a proposal by a creditor does not release any person who would not be released under this Act by the discharge of the debtor.

Default in performance of proposal

62.1 Where

(a) default is made in the performance of any provision in a proposal,

(b) the default is not waived

　　(i) by the inspectors, or

　　(ii) if there are no inspectors, by the creditors, and

(c) the default is not remedied by the insolvent person within the prescribed time,

the trustee shall, within such time and in such form and manner as are prescribed, so inform all the creditors and the official receiver.

Receiving order on default, etc.

63. (1) Where default is made in the performance of any provision in a proposal, or where it appears to the court that the proposal cannot continue without injustice or undue delay or that the approval of the court was obtained by fraud, the court may, on application thereto, with such notice as the court may direct to the debtor, and, if applicable to the trustee and to the creditors, annul the proposal.

Validity of things done

(2) An order made under subsection (1) shall be made without prejudice to the validity of any sale, disposition of property or payment duly made, or anything duly done under or in pursuance of the proposal, and notwithstanding the annulment of the proposal, a guarantee given pursuant to the proposal remains in full force and effect in accordance with its terms.

Annulment for offence

(3) A proposal, although accepted or approved, may be annulled by order of the court at the request of the trustee or of any creditor whenever the debtor is afterwards convicted of any offence under this Act.

Effect of annulling order

(4) On the annulment of a proposal, the debtor shall be deemed to have thereupon made an assignment and the order annulling the proposal shall so state.

Meeting of creditors to be called

(5) Where an order annulling a proposal has been made, the trustee shall, within five days after the order is made, send notice of the meeting of creditors under section 102, at which meeting the creditors may by ordinary resolution, notwithstanding section 14, affirm the appointment of the trustee or appoint another licensed trustee in lieu of that trustee.

Consequences of annulment

(6) Where an order annulling the proposal described in subsection (5) has been made, the trustee shall forthwith file a report thereof in the prescribed form with the official receiver, who shall thereupon issue a certificate of assignment in the prescribed form, which has the same effect for the purposes of this Act as an assignment filed pursuant to section 49.

Assignment pending court approval of proposal

64. For greater certainty, where an insolvent person in respect of whom a notice of intention has been filed under section 50.4 or a proposal has been filed under section 62 makes an assignment at any time before the court has approved the proposal, the date of the bankruptcy is the date of the filing of the assignment.

Where proposal is conditional on purchase of new securities

65. A proposal made conditional on the purchase of shares or securities or on any other payment or contribution by the

creditors shall provide that the claim of any creditor who elects not to participate in the proposal shall be valued by the court and shall be paid in cash on approval of the proposal.

Certain rights limited

65.1 (1) Where a notice of intention or a proposal has been filed in respect of an insolvent person, no person may terminate or amend any agreement with the insolvent person, or claim an accelerated payment under any agreement with the insolvent person, by reason only that

(a) the insolvent person is insolvent; or

(b) a notice of intention or a proposal has been filed in respect of the insolvent person.

Idem

(2) Where the agreement referred to in subsection (1) is a lease or a licensing agreement, subsection (1) shall be read as including the following paragraph:

"(c) the insolvent person has not paid rent or royalties, as the case may be, or other payments of a similar nature, in respect of a period preceding the filing of

(i) the notice of intention, if one was filed, or

(ii) the proposal, if no notice of intention was filed."

Idem

(3) Where a notice of intention or a proposal has been filed in respect of an insolvent person, no public utility may

discontinue service to that insolvent person by reason only that

(a) the insolvent person is insolvent;

(b) a notice of intention or a proposal has been filed in respect of the insolvent person; or

(c) the insolvent person has not paid for services rendered, or material provided, before the filing of

    (i) the notice of intention, if one was filed, or

    (ii) the proposal, if no notice of intention was filed.

Certain acts not prevented

(4) Nothing in subsections (1) to (3) shall be construed

(a) as prohibiting a person from requiring immediate payment for goods, services, use of leased or licensed property or other valuable consideration provided after the filing of

    (i) the notice of intention, if one was filed, or

    (ii) the proposal, if no notice of intention was filed; or

(b) as requiring the further advance of money or credit.

Provisions of section override agreement

(5) Any provision in an agreement that has the effect of providing for, or permitting, anything that, in substance, is contrary to subsections (1) to (3) is of no force or effect.

Powers of court

(6) The court may, on application by a party to an agreement or by a public utility, declare that subsections (1) to (3) do

not apply, or apply only to the extent declared by the court, where the applicant satisfies the court that the operation of those subsections would likely cause it significant financial hardship.

Eligible financial contracts

(7) Subsection (1) does not apply

(a) in respect of an eligible financial contract; or
(b) to prevent a member of the Canadian Payments Association established by the Canadian Payments Association Act from ceasing to act as a clearing agent or group clearer for an insolvent person in accordance with that Act and the by-laws and rules of that Association.

Definitions

(8) In subsections (7) and (9),
« contrat financier admissible »
"eligible financial contract" means

(a) a currency or interest rate swap agreement,

(b) a basis swap agreement,

(c) a spot, future, forward or other foreign exchange agreement,

(d) a cap, collar or floor transaction,

(e) a commodity swap,

(f) a forward rate agreement,

(g) a repurchase or reverse repurchase agreement,

(h) a spot, future, forward or other commodity contract,

(i) an agreement to buy, sell, borrow or lend securities, to clear or settle securities transactions or to act as a depository for securities,

(j) any derivative, combination or option in respect of, or agreement similar to, an agreement or contract referred to in paragraphs (a) to (i),

(k) any master agreement in respect of any agreement or contract referred to in paragraphs (a) to (j),

(k.1) any master agreement in respect of a master agreement referred to in paragraph (k),

(l) a guarantee of the liabilities under an agreement or contract referred to in paragraphs (a) to (k.1), or

(m) any agreement of a kind prescribed;

"net termination value"

« valeurs nettes dues à la date de résiliation »

"net termination value" means the net amount obtained after setting off the mutual obligations between the parties to an eligible financial contract in accordance with its provisions.

Application of paragraphs 69(1)(a) and 69.1(1)(a)

(9) For greater certainty, where an eligible financial contract entered into before the filing in respect of an insolvent person of

(a) a notice of intention, or

(b) a proposal, where no notice of intention was filed, is terminated on or after that filing, the setting off of obligations between the insolvent person and the other parties to the eligible financial contract, in accordance with its provisions, shall be permitted, and if net termination values determined in accordance with the eligible financial contract are owed by the insolvent person to another party to the eligible financial contract, that other party shall be deemed, for the purposes of paragraphs 69(1)(a) and 69.1(1)(a), to be a creditor of the insolvent person with a claim provable in bankruptcy in respect of those net termination values.

Insolvent person may disclaim commercial lease
65.2 (1) At any time between the filing of a notice of intention and the filing of a proposal, or on the filing of a proposal, in respect of an insolvent person who is a commercial tenant under a lease of real property, the insolvent person may disclaim the lease on giving thirty days notice to the landlord in the prescribed manner, subject to subsection (2).

Landlord may challenge
(2) Within fifteen days after being given notice of the disclaimer of a lease under subsection (1), the landlord may apply to the court for a declaration that subsection (1) does not apply in respect of that lease, and the court, on notice to such parties as it may direct, shall, subject to subsection (3), make such a declaration.

Where no declaration to be made
(3) No declaration under subsection (2) shall be made if the

court is satisfied that the insolvent person would not be able to make a viable proposal without the disclaimer of the lease and all other leases that the tenant has disclaimed under subsection (1).

Effects of disclaimer

(4) Where a lease is disclaimed under subsection (1),

(a) the landlord has no claim for accelerated rent;
(b) the proposal must indicate whether the landlord may file a proof of claim for the actual losses resulting from the disclaimer, or for an amount equal to the lesser of

    (i) the aggregate of

        (A) the rent provided for in the lease for the first year of the lease following the date on which the disclaimer becomes effective, and

        (B) fifteen per cent of the rent for the remainder of the term of the lease after that year, and

    (ii) three years' rent; and

(c) the landlord may file a proof of claim as indicated in the proposal.

Classification of claim

(5) The landlord's claim shall be included in either

(a) a separate class of similar claims of landlords; or
(b) a class of unsecured claims that includes claims of creditors who are not landlords.

Landlord's vote on proposal

(6) The landlord is entitled to vote on the proposal in whichever class referred to in subsection (5) the landlord's claim is included, and for the amount of the claim as proven.

Determination of classes

(7) The court may, on application made at any time after the proposal is filed, determine the classes of claims of landlords and the class into which any particular landlord's claim falls.

Section 146 not affected

(8) Nothing in subsections (1) to (7) affects the operation of section 146 in the event of bankruptcy.

Lease disclaimer where tenant is a bankrupt

65.21 Where, in respect of a proposal concerning a bankrupt person who is a commercial tenant under a lease of real property, the tenant's lease has been surrendered or disclaimed in the bankruptcy proceedings, subsections 65.2(3) to (7) apply in the same manner and to the same extent as if the person was not a bankrupt but was an insolvent person in respect of which a disclaimer referred to in those subsections applies.

Bankruptcy after court approval

65.22 Where an insolvent person who has disclaimed a lease under subsection 65.2(1) becomes bankrupt after the court approval of the proposal and before the proposal is fully performed, any claim of the landlord in respect of losses resulting from the disclaimer, including any claim for accelerated rent, shall be reduced by the amount of compensation paid under the proposal for losses resulting from the disclaimer.

Certificate where proposal performed

65.3 Where a proposal is fully performed, the trustee shall give a certificate to that effect, in the prescribed form, to the debtor and to the official receiver.

Act to apply

66. (1) All the provisions of this Act, except Division II of this Part, in so far as they are applicable, apply, with such modifications as the circumstances require, to proposals made under this Division.

Effect of Companies' Creditors Arrangement Act

(2) Notwithstanding the Companies' Creditors Arrangement Act,

(a) proceedings commenced under that Act shall not be dealt with or continued under this Act; and
(b) proceedings shall not be commenced under Part III of this Act in respect of a company if a compromise or arrangement has been proposed in respect of the company under the Companies' Creditors Arrangement Act and the compromise or arrangement has not been agreed to by the creditors or sanctioned by the court under that Act.

CALL THE AUTHOR

(416) 463-9440

Frank S. Kisluk

PRESIDENT
DEBTOR CONSULTING SERVICES LTD.

VICE-PRESIDENT
MANDELBAUM SPERGEL INC.
TRUSTEE IN BANKRUPTCY

307A Danforth Avenue
Toronto, Ontario M4K 1N7

Fax: (416) 778-6016
e-mail: frank@msg.ca
http://www.debtorconsulting.com